ANNE PIA's creative memoir *Language of My Choosing* was shortlisted for the Saltire Award for Best New Book of 2017. In 2018, Anne was awarded the Premio Italiano Linguistica. With the assistance of funding from Publishing Scotland the Italian translation *Ho Scelto La Mia Lingua* was published in 2018 by MnM edizioni. Her first poetry collection, *Transitory*, was published in 2018. Anne's poetry and essays have appeared in among others, *The Blue Nib*, *Northwords Now*, *Poetry Scotland*, *Lunar Poetry*, *The Fat Damsel* and London's *South Bank Poetry* magazine. Anne has appeared at the Dundee Literary Festival and the Stanza International Poetry Festival and has done events in venues across Scotland including the Scottish Storytelling Centre, the National Library of Scotland, the City Art Centre, Glasgow Women's Library and the Italian Cultural Institute in Edinburgh. In 2018 she was invited to the British Institute in Florence and to the Torino Book Festival in 2019 to showcase her book.

Pia shows us that pilgrimages to places of the past are important stations to stop at, but planning the next odyssey into the future of possibilities can also be beneficial... JANETTE AYACHI

Keeping Away the Spiders *is lyrical and candid... brimming with insight, poetry and music.* SANDRA IRELAND

[Transitory *is] a beautifully eloquent mission of direct communication across the differences that give us identities.* ALAN RIACH

[poems of] *honesty and bluntness, as social convention is blown apart* CHRISTINE DE LUCA

Language of My Choosing *is book that will challenge its readers to ear up all the scripts society has written for us and find their own words...* RICHARD HOLLOWAY

By the same author:

Language of My Choosing Luath Press, 2017
Transitory (poetry) Luath Press, 2018

Keeping Away the Spiders

essays on breaching barriers

ANNE PIA

Luath Press Limited

EDINBURGH

www.luath.co.uk

First published 2020

ISBN: 978-1-913025-72-4

The paper used in this book is recyclable. It is made
from low chlorine pulps produced in a low energy,
low emission manner from renewable forests.

Printed and bound by Bell & Bain Ltd, Glasgow

Typeset in 12 point Sabon and Noteworthy
by Main Point Books, Edinburgh

A special dedication to my little granddaughter Stevie Iris, to my daughters, Camilla, Roberta and Sophie-Louise and to Geraldine whose love and humour keep me journeying.

contents

acknowledgements

I want to thank the following for their endless support and encouragement: Sheila, Aileen and Marian, and for excellent and honest commentaries at the crucial stages... Tamsin, Laura, Linda, Izzy and Sean. My special thanks as ever to Jennie Renton and to Carrie Hutchison, my editor.

author's note

I finished writing this book in early January 2020 when the pandemic loomed, but was still for me an unknown and far off. I wrote it in order to share my thoughts, to start a conversation about survival. I wanted to celebrate possibility, freedom, joy. I wanted to speak up for hope and optimism because, even in my darkest times, I live my life believing in these things.

The speed of the change in our lives as a result of the pandemic has been both shocking and humbling, confronting us with the things we can't control. In the early days of lockdown, this book that I so believed in, no longer mattered and I grieved for it. I grieved for lost words and for vanished worlds. Most of all, I feared the future and everything around me that was outside my familiar. In bleakest lockdown, like millions of others, I took careful stock of my mental and physical vulnerabilities. I realised with unprecedented starkness, how flimsy and precious my hold is on my emotional stability, my own life and those of the people I care about; then slowly, through unexpected significances of my different every day, a smile or an ice cream cone, I did find new small, safe and happy spaces.

At this time more than ever, as we move into a new era, I believe and hope that these pages will steady, inspire, give confidence in possibility, confirm and reawaken the ingenuity and creativity that we possess, the innate and discrete capacities that we have, that help us not only to live and live fully, but to enjoy, flourish and maybe even grow a tiny bit taller.

Anne Pia

October 2020

opener

... as I lie in bed alone, I consider the spider that may be lurking underneath the bed frame. I see a large black shape, fast moving, as loose in her movements as a dusting cloth. This spider has some power over me. She hears my breath. Our movements co-ordinate. With each shift of my position she is alerted. In dodging my gaze she renders me completely paralysed. She is skilled in subterfuge; with a wide range of vision as she scans her surroundings; and hydrostatic impetus in her every move – at once still and then quickly out of nowhere, and then away. In these lone moments, I am unable to keep at bay the thoughts that linger around the edges of each day and of almost every joyful moment... the fearful, unremitting blackness of dying, plunged unexpectedly and in a flash into the void; a sudden, thudding body splitting blow from nowhere as I make my bed or dry my hair; or being eased gently with the help of drugs, against any decisive will of my own, into a terrible pitch black. I will have some minutes maybe, to assess what has taken place, my brain will question, scream and burn its panic, and then along with realisation, my brain function will slow to stop. Then nothing. The feeling of nothing. And I reject this imminent nothingness.

It is always the same: once you are liberated, you are forced to ask who you are.

(Jean Baudrillard)

I do not know who I am: Who are you? I often ask myself as I take in the streets of my city, the sound of church bells, wash the windows of my flat or ride a bus to the gym. Am I happy or a pathological depressive? Passionate, generous of heart or mean with my money? Arrogant and self-promoting or self-doubting and choked with anxiety? An irrepressible optimist or suffocatingly morbid? Am I an idealist, a romantic, caring and sensitive, empathetic and loving or a forensically cut-throat calculator, vengeful and envious; sometimes a brutal psychopath even, baying for blood? Would I resort to violence or am I the essence of finessed restraint? Would I declare myself spiritual or a selfish pleasure-seeking Hedonist? Is it the strength or the weakness in me that people see? A bully or meekly compliant?

The reality is that I am and have been all of these conflicting things and much, much more – a contradiction – as variable and complex as the chemistry of spice in a curry. And how much of what others say of us can we trust, should we take seriously? The determining factor, what defines or frames us is mainly external. The circumstances that are imposed on us or the situations that we choose. Who we are is often reactive and improvised within a given environment. We are unreliable. We continually construct and deconstruct, reconstruct and mutate. In the absence of our interaction or engagement with a set of circumstances, when all human contact is swept away, who are we then and what remains?

I believe that while we continually build, adapt and remake our identity, there is an aspect or thread which exists, irrespective of the words or actions of other people; an essential core, which is not brought into being by an external force, but is an enduring self-determining energy which drives us to continually build variable, sometimes competing, new identities. Christians might still refer to it as free will.

It is that vibrant surge, that often eclectic push of self-moving that wakes me some mornings with such a love of the physical world, its diversity, its mysteries and rewards, finds me so full of lust for life that I could, if my legs weren't so short, my pace too slow, stride Colossus-like across the earth's entirety in a day, place a foot in every continent and ride the waves of each of the earth's great oceans.

There are occasions too when my day to day is not enough and I look for ways of living another life on a bigger, broader scale; when I need to expand beyond limits, when it is the big world stage that I seek.

There are days too, when I want to live on an altogether different level, to travel across London with nothing but an Oyster card and not a penny in my pocket to replace it should I accidentally drop it, to drive a luxury car, have afternoon tea wearing a hat or limit myself, for want of better, to a dinner of corned beef and tortillas in a small tent.

And I willingly throw myself into the unknown, take on new selves, impelled by basic instinct simply

Only one who takes over his own life history can see it in the realisation of his self. Responsibility to take over one's own biography means to get clear about who one wants to be. (Habermas)

because I just want to keep on becoming.

This book is not a memoir. It is an assertion about identity, about who we are, who we can become and the opportunities in our lives for transformation. All my experience in educating young people and adults returning to learning has taught me that safe, valuing learning environments can lead to fundamental, personal change and that transformation is always possible. I am convinced too by Buddhist philosophy together with events in my own life, that we live in a world where nothing is fixed or solid. Everything is impermanent and will pass. We therefore conduct our lives, broken threads against an unreliable background of constant change, continual motion, which require us to keep adapting in response. We gain, lose, choose, recycle and self-create through what we learn from others, what of theirs we value, through the lifestyles we choose and important decisions that we take, and in how we react to those major and unforeseen events that often overtake us and that we find ourselves confronted with.

In this book, I have drawn mainly on autobiographical material. The collages which follow are unrelated and inconsistent; as non-sequential and random as life. They serve as examples. In showing the extent of my own personal shift, reconfigurations, responses and reframing, the struggles, the gains, the ever-present shifting star just within reach, my purpose is to share what I have learned; to offer a certain philosophy and to comment on wider social and political issues in the world as I understand them.

reluctant feminist

... she had the habit of keeping a basin under the bed and a nightly ritual of wiping her vagina with a wet cloth before settling down beside me, where unable to move or turn, though both fascinated and repulsed at the same time, I tried not to look. Silent, I hugged the margin of the mattress. Throughout my entire six-week stay at that house, the practice continued.

For some reason I remember those summer days in Italy in 1967 as pink days. I wore quite a lot of it and the youthfulness of the palest of colours counteracted the sluggishness that seemed to grip everyone in the house after lunch. I hated that time of day, everyone heavy, drugged with food and homemade wine poured from Coca-Cola bottles, and asleep; every bed full, mouths open, bodies slack, left to rumble, gurgle and wheeze, right in the middle of a fine, fine day, glorious before its leisurely cadencing to late afternoon and dusk.

I wasn't meant to be there really, in that small Italian village near Atina. At the age of 17, just out of boarding school, I found myself in the Italian Lake District. And after several days of feeling lonely and increasingly anxious and frightened, I had to be rescued from suicidal depression. To my relief, I was carried off by my mother's young man, at her fervent request, to his sister's home in Ponte Melfa near Sora in the central Appennine Mountains. He deposited me in the safe-keeping of his sister and mother like a man bringing home the war-wounded. Which in a way I was. His mother then became my bedfellow. I still remember the soft grey of Garda's lake, high on the banking, imagining its tender embrace, all fears vanishing as I gratefully let myself go, thankful of its depths. So, there I was in rural Italy, tall and substantial, outlandishly Scottish in manner and dress, lumpen and lacking any of the guile of a country Italian girl, but with a southern *laziale* dialect, the authenticity of which astonished the entire village.

I came home to Edinburgh after six weeks of stretching out on the Coppola family's roof terrace, roasting in the fiery sunshine. I was about to start university, deemed by the world able for life but I had been distinctly unable to deal with sex, innuendo, a lustful gaze, the brush of a fingertip. Which is why I had to be rescued. Why I panicked to the point of walking through a glass window one afternoon and in those days, lying awake at night, fearful of someone standing outside my bedroom door listening. So, we maintained, my mother and I, the pretence of a successful summer school, for which I had truthfully won a bursary from the Italian Department of Edinburgh University, but never got as far as a classroom desk.

I was in hiding in Italy, all thoughts of my exclusive study programme banished. How would I explain my failures to a prospective professor? I was sleeping with the matronly mother of my mother's boyfriend. I still wonder to this day, since he had not, I assume, given any account of the circumstances of his connection to my family, how he had persuaded his people to take me in.

Nothing had prepared me for a priest whom I automatically assumed to be chaste and God- fearing, conditioned as I was by the nuns that educated me to trust the wisdom of a dog collar. After a drink at our first meeting in Milan and some minutes in his car – he had been commissioned by my aunt to meet and drive me to my destination in Garda – he pointedly removed his dog collar and announced his freedom. And nothing had prepared me for the man sitting opposite me with his wife, all of us on the pontoon stretching over the lake, who on my first afternoon after my arrival at my *pensione*, suggested while she disappeared indoors, that I shave the pubic hair escaping from the edges around my prim swimsuit.

Up until that moment, I had never considered my pubic hair. Apart from a general look around that area, I had paid it scarce attention. But the sexual messages from these two men, my first experience of males outside my family circle, made me feel vulnerable and insecure. My inability to find words, to adopt a convincing expression or pose which might counter such intrusive behaviour left me feeling gauche, unattractive and ugly. I was rendered inferior, reduced, lost in a place that I did not understand, that I did not have the language or skills for.

There is a welcome honesty today in relation to unsolicited sexual attention and harassment and my problem was partly a generational one, part of an era well gone. I applaud women who have grown in confidence to the point where uninvited male attention is named, exposed and condemned. I glory in women who do not seek definition by men, who make their own choices, who are generally pretty confident of how they look, their attractiveness, who are not drawn in by the words, sideways glances or behaviours of men. And I regret not having had that strength and resilience. But I needed admiration and compliments. I needed that attention in order to feel okay.

My feminism was never in question, it came naturally and was well rooted. But it was my behaviour, my decisions and neediness which compromised it, disguised it or betrayed it. I have still not forgiven the boys I mixed with when I was about to leave school for fancying each of my school friends while I didn't match up. Was it something that they saw or did not see in me? Was I so different? Was there some game at work that I hadn't quite understood?

There was one boy that I really liked called Mark and I told my best friend. After arriving later than expected at a party, I was surprised when they opened the door to me clearly together. I was stung on both counts. I learned that even when friendship is deep, it is no match for sexual game-play. When it comes to the love tangle, it will always trump friendship, leaving you suddenly bereft.

Even now, a lifetime later, when his or her name comes up, I still feel a small stab of pain. My anger and shame still a pinprick. It was a determining event. If I wasn't able to compete in the arena of sexual attraction, I could mercilessly compete in all the others areas of my life. A new driving energy had sprung into being and has lasted to this day. Some of those boys have crossed my path since, as elderly and mature men.

My response has been cool.

As a child, I never for one moment considered myself in any way less than my male cousins, and as an adult, never less than male colleagues, than the husbands of friends, or indeed inferior to my own husband. My difficulty arose rather from my lack of self-belief both intellectually and as a woman. My mother had always told me that I was special and different to other people, but I didn't believe it. She used those words more as an exhortation to do the right thing, whatever that was. Her intention was to make me conform to norms and expectations. So, faced with a man, rather than assert, I either punctured his soliloquy or I adopted a grateful, submissive approach, listening to his orations, deferring to his pronouncements as infallible, as this approach offered some stability in a world I was discovering but did not understand. I performed the femininity expected of me. Male attention had passed me by as a teenager but overwhelmed me when I played the game of the flirtacious, second-class being who flattered egos and satisfied male need for being central to any conversation or gathering.

I still see young women who carry the values and stigma of my diffident generation of women who mothered them, who are complimented when a man touches them without consent and who regard an invitation to drinks, bed or a club as affirmation of their attractiveness. But more and more, there is an intolerance of sexual subjugation; an intolerance of a lack of respect for womanhood, women's choices and women's needs. The impatience I see among women in relation to male dominance, men putting their needs first, is now spoken, acted upon and illegalised. We are witnessing a massive showdown, a reckoning. With the unveiling and vocalising of female experiences, historic and present day, across the Western world, there is public shaming of furtive, forward, ignorantly impudent, dodoesque menfolk. We both and not just you, will agree the terms of this engagement across the sexual divide. And if I dress in a way that you think is provocative or inviting, I do so not to impress or excite you but because I want to feel like a woman for myself. I want to enhance my own sexual appetite and fanciful imaginings. My presentation is my ritual, my identity and my chosen currency. It has nothing whatsoever to do with you.

I have not been a good feminist. I recognise this. Susie Orbach, Judith Butler, Roxane Gay, Caitlin Moran, Mary Beard, for example, and worthy authors of such books as *Reclaiming the F Word* and *Come as You Are,* might well despise my cowardice. While in the '70s, my good sisters were claiming ownership of their bodies and equal status with men, I was not only swaddled in middle class wifeliness, which despite my professional journey, I was happy to inhabit, but I was critical of the politics and iterations of that second wave of feminism.

There are, of course, mitigating circumstances. As an Italian Scot, having arrived in a competitive world and gaining promotions over men, having travelled from the counter of a café/ice cream shop, leaving the rawness of an immigrant family behind, I did not, would never then take, what I saw as a backward step to left wing extremism, to presentations of myself as a woman who could not afford better because that was too close to where I had come from. My social foothold was not yet entirely secure, my birthright still only a breath away. My purpose was to display what I had fashioned for myself, to parade what I could afford. I had lived and done the other. That breadbin with our Christmas money, salvaged from the pubs that my pitiful, drunken father visited, the screaming disagreements and hair pulling, all were not far enough away. I found then, that capitulating to the norm, giving way to role stereotyping, relaxing into society's expectations of womanhood was not only easier but undemanding and very pleasant. In that there was an order about it. No confrontations, no hard edges. My nights were peaceful, my days untroubled by any thoughts other than planning my next lesson, the contents of my freezer and how to fill a cheeseboard.

Though while I indulged a superficial, materialistic identity, I remained at all times, starkly realistic about myself and my lifestyle. I knew what I was doing; I had made the easy choice. So the battle was won by others while I fiddled, so busy was I to make, feather and gild my nest. It was maybe easier to stand for a cause from a firm middle class footing at that time. But so much braver to challenge sexism, class and elitism when you are financially and socially vulnerable, to articulate and pursue your beliefs when those around you, men and women may see you as motivated by envy and anger.

I am not sure at what point my feminist revolt began. My family background had a great deal to do with it. The men that surrounded me as a child were violent and ominous and I saw strong women degraded by them. As I grew up, I became more and more enraged by those power relations, observing the submissiveness of women who ultimately crumbled before their might.

My husband on the other hand, was a civil, happy and loving man, courteous and calm and our home was a welcome oasis, a delightful respite after those earlier years. I remember a scene in one of Ferrante's novels where a father throws his daughter out of the window in temper, thus breaking her arm. This has stayed in my mind. While no limbs were broken in my childhood home, this distressing, crude display was not unfamiliar. As a newly married woman it often seemed that I was two people: when confronted by a family situation, it was hard to maintain dignity and composure, and I descended to a level that I was and am not proud of; back in my own space, hours later, I was the essence of self-styled, middle class refinement and good behaviour.

While family on both sides acknowledged my career choice, it became clear that they had no appreciation of my aspirations and at any mention of promotion or moving on, I detected a slight unease, a discreet change of subject towards more domestic matters. Clearly the expectation was that as a wife and mother primarily, my role was to support and enable my husband's career advancement. Self-sacrifice was a woman's lot.

Not long after the birth of my second child, we went on holiday to Italy with my mother. I was still struggling with post-natal depression which no one seemed to notice and which only my GP knew about. After what had been a difficult and exhausting car journey to a beautiful Tuscan resort, I woke up one morning feeling crushed and lonely. There was no one who made me feel valued or cherished. I had been assigned a role that I did not want and that was not me. I was 35 and I felt as if my life was over, submerged as I was within the patriarchal structure I grew up in and married into. I wanted more from life, I demanded more and I knew that I was capable of better.

My subsequent and decisive move out of the school system into wider, more prominent roles in education was significant. In doing so, I left well behind me the traditions and norms of Catholic education and those of family and community. Liberated from those repressive attitudes, active on a bigger stage, I began to meet and mix more widely. I was influenced by able women who were independent, whose work commitments and the impact of responsibility had equal currency within the family structure, women who conducted their lives very differently to what I had been used to. The dismal staff room chat among Catholic wives about Rome and bishop-approved methods of birth control and how to make good 'stovies' for the men, coming home hungry after football, were well behind me. Instead of hosting or attending Sunday lunches with extended family, these other women went to the gym or a sauna to relax after a demanding week, they met friends for lunch or went to an art gallery or wrote papers on a Sunday night about policy and educational development. Better still, they took trips away with friends. In Italian eyes, it would have been outrageous and negligent for a mother of three to behave in that way and particularly for a mother who was scarcely at home through the week, albeit working.

As I grew in confidence, feeling increasingly able and free, I challenged the settled status quo at home. I stopped the dinner parties, and the *duck à l'orange*, replacing them with walking boots. I started smoking cigars and I finally ventured full of fear, into the feminist and lesbian community. I started to protest at offensive male behaviour, oracles and dogma. To my astonishment however, if the heterosexual world demanded conformity, the radical feminists and the lesbians were not far from that mark either. Not for them the brave new frontiers of sexual behaviour, of gender bending, androgyny and sexual fluidity. Had I wanted to indulge in it, polyamory would certainly not have won me many friends. I found the Scottish lesbian community uncompromising and illiberal, with set rules for living, bizarrely replicating heterosexual patterns with clearly assigned roles, protocols and uniforms. To me, feminists were often loudly radical, angry and unrelenting. I had hoped for open-mindedness, liberalism and creativity, a community of individuals defining their lifestyles, non-hierarchical in the manner Marge Piercy imagined in her amazing *Woman on the Edge of Time*.

Having dreamed of a network where I might meet brave, like-minded women (for these women had been brave indeed in asserting their sexuality), somewhat bruised, I retreated. By my love of clothes, fashion, make-up and large, dare I say, sophisticated gatherings around my table (I favoured whole artichokes dipped in a wonderful vinaigrette rather than a humble pie and beans), by my love of classical music, my enjoyment of the company of both men and women, I stood judged, both by feminists of the '70s and '80s that I met, and who would have preferred me threadbare rather than clad in Jaeger tailoring, and lesbians who would probably have taken to me more readily had I deserted my husband, home and children but would have despised me for abandoning my cat, had I owned one. My closest relationships have though, always been with women, the closest fit emotionally and instinctively; my even closer relationships have been with my daughters.

Two years ago, I was reading from my memoir and poetry collection in London. In order to open up the discussion, my eldest daughter asked if I would call myself a feminist. 'Oh no!' I said, 'I don't like labels.' Aware that I had not met the challenge she set me in public, I was shamed. Since then, with her occasional guidance, I have made it my objective to read some of the literature and poetry around the current feminist wave. To my sheer delight, I found a language, an outlook on life, a way of seeing the world, a way of both understanding, being with and countering men which had silently been developing within my own consciousness and mind as an academic, a professional and more recently as a writer. The discovery was both empowering and overpowering.

My reading in preparation for my doctoral thesis had aroused my awareness of feminist qualitative research methodology and of the gendering of practices, systems and institutions. From the gender balance on Boards of Trustees, to the bank clerk who welcomes every man with a respectful 'sir' and softens his tone when addressing a woman; from the man who tells you about a wonderful book he has read, the book you yourself wrote, and continues to tell you, despite your protestations that you are actually the author; from the erudite man to whom you have spoken about your recent research into Mary Queen of Scots at a local gathering of Edinburgh poets who provides an improvised, on the spot lecture on her; from the statuary in and around my city, almost all of men, some distinguished, some less so; to the disturbing hum of masculinity, the high constables and the archers of Edinburgh, with their bows and arrows providing the guard of honour at formal occasions in Holyroodhouse, and at any royal or significant public event such as the Queen's Garden Party, and the illustrious male personage who carries the Mace or the Purse at the Scottish Parliament.

That academic preparation also awakened me to the patriarchy which I had long experienced working within government, making me ultimately generally mutinous within my organisation. The lack of self-doubt or open, intellectual enquiry that I saw in the men around me infuriated me. Equally, I became quick to detect the professional weakness which underlies mansplaining, and prompt in emboldening and supporting fellow female, able professionals, encouraging them to go forward in their careers.

As a mature woman, with the honesty that comes with age and achievement, with no need to be defined by men, or indeed women, I find I now am finally equipped to meet men on equal terms. Both to dispense compliments and to be gracious in receipt of them. Most importantly, I am now not only ready but most anxious to embrace, despite it all, whatever is imagined, invented, is said, unsaid or known about me – by the scarved woman in French cotton upstairs, the testosterone-loaded men with cash in their back pockets who find me unsettling, by the symbiotic couples whose horizons stop at each other, by the smoothly intoning mummies drinking lattes in buggyland and by the communities I visited but was never part of – ultimately by the 'sisterhood', that F word which once gave me such nightmares.

Very recently, I attended the funeral of a cousin

of my husband's. My husband and I separated some years ago but are close friends and, after a lifetime, our differences honed by the rub and grit of years, we are still family to one another in certain situations. The gradual breakdown of our marriage has not changed our ability to communicate and reach, usually, some common agreement or understanding. As we approached the gathering outside the church where all of his close family were assembled, he took my arm, greeted people and led me to the pews where his siblings and partners were seated. We lead different lives now, coming together to celebrate events that involve our three daughters, formulating strategy when one of them requires support of any kind and of course taking the time to support each other. But that gesture of intimacy in that public setting said a great deal. It gave a strong message to those around us seeking something to chew on and placed me still at the centre of the family that he and I created together and of whom we are so proud and thankful.

The expectations and judgements of others, of our communities should neither phase or inhibit us from being who we are or want to become. Normal and acceptable behaviour is behaviour which neither disturbs or unsettles you or those who are important to you. What others outwith that group consider to be normal or acceptable is of no concern. We must be ever vigilant about societal pressure and a prevailing culture which is covert and unspoken. As individuals who must take ultimate responsibility for our own destiny, I believe that we must follow our own instincts and feelings, for they are what matter, and assess carefully the burdens we carry, in order to reach the place that we want to be. With wisdom, knowledge and empathy we find how and to what extent we can manoeuvre and move forward. Because everything passes and melts away, timing and positioning in our journey are crucial.

insight

... it was a stark kitchen even though the sun had risen and the corners and crevices had begun to respond to filtering light. We had been up all night. Cold but joyful all four of us, three friends from university and I, had breakfasted on hot chocolate and warm croissants in a brasserie somewhere near the river after waiting for the dawn. I was excited, having a sense of Paris, a first visit and a first insight. I was in my early 20s, fresh from Edinburgh University with a degree in languages. This was not Florence or London and certainly not anywhere in Scotland.

Paris is a city where the unreal becomes possible; the home of fantasists, bohemians and artistes, where all are able, like nowhere else in the world, to conjure up and live different realities. It is a city of idiosyncrasy, of burlesque and masks; and at the same time, of ordinary folk with shopping bags and neat, brightly coloured trolleys, of slim-suited men with carefully brushed hair, carrying fine leather briefcases, of long-legged young women of colour, outstanding in plain black tailoring, of alleyways where black 25 or something year-olds, immigrant and discarded, play ball, of expansive boulevards and neat parks. Paris summons buried and unbidden fragments of the mind, conjures up what is never spoken, brings back what is disowned, makes visible the ugly, the unnamed and downright outrageous. It tolerates iterations of who you might want to be or who you are in reality. Those figments from your personal no-mans-land, of that private place between your waking and sleeping, where the indescribable and the unsayable normally hang out, are catered to and even cherished. Paris is a city where it is not unusual to request a meal at 4.00am, where a Pagliacci figure, or a man with a parrot on his shoulder can walk into a café deep in Montparnasse and order a bottle of champagne in the small hours, where a brandy with your breakfast mussels is respectable, where even now a box of cigars is unquestioningly brought to a table of women and where a homeless *chanteuse de rue* will work the terraces of a *petit resto* and literally sing for her supper. All are unremarkable. All are Paris. If you want it to be.

The four people at the table next to ours were in post-party mood. They were drinking champagne at 4.00am. My friends and I, on the other hand, had spent the evening differently. About to leave for Scotland the following morning, three of us, but not Cécile who had moved from her home in the Auvergne to live and study at the Ecole Nationale Supérieure des Beaux-Arts in Paris, had been intent on collecting last cameos of the city that we could pocket and store for the foreseeable future... a lifetime even.

Suddenly we were all back at the flat. I have no memory of how we got there nor indeed of leaving the bar. But a look had been exchanged between us, familiar, understood, and so, each of us noiselessly made our way, from the rooms each of us was sharing with one of the other girls. We had been very careful not to share together. It was the early '70s and a different era. Paris permitted in part; whereas young women with 'respectable' backgrounds from Presbyterian Scotland, had not yet seen enough of the world. Without those boundaries we would have given it away. Maybe it was obvious already.

Finally, I was standing in front of her. Me, warm and unsure with a year's living since an earlier time in France; a year which had not included her. I was heavy with decision. She, solid, as I always remembered her, her lips wet. Like the first and many other times since. All night we had promised each other these private hours, across tables, rooms, heads, hands... as we walked, as we chatted, as we obligingly laughed. We had caught something of each other in the air. There we were now, eventually, in a kitchen which was altogether too clean, too metallic and far too ordered. We said little, overcome with both the familiarity and strangeness of each other; the need to make no noise; an awareness of our separate destinies after this last night. And so our touching was contained and chaste; reminiscent of another goodbye 12 months before.

'I am going to marry', was all I said.

That earlier leaving of Cécile on a public platform where I climbed aboard a train for London, my stubborn legs slow and resistant to the necessity of keeping on walking, my gaze still holding her for as long as I could, en route for a home where Cécile would be denied and my own reality would be silent. Now frail, on that platform, in an instant reduced, but stoic, Cécile had watched my departure from the *Gare du Nord* and always formal in the ways of the French, gathered her grief into herself, afraid of drawing attention, causing comment. She never knew about my deep shame at loving her, of my years of fear of discovery, that would turn my insides to ice; my memories of how she would look at me fiercely and the stirring that took the strength from my limbs and made me stumble; of the slow, sad holding of each other in that dining room in the *Rue des Arbousiers* to the music of Ennio Morricone on our last meagre days together, inevitability clouding the dwindling, sweet time we had left; of the continual imagining of her laugh, that gave away something of her roots in the deep alluvial valleys of the *Tarn*; of her stiff, unbending gait, always a bewildered look behind sensible glasses; those ways of hers that me so tender, made me tremble for years after. She never knew, I never told her, how I was unable to find any rest, unable to slow the pace of a life which I created in order not to think of her. A hurly-burly lifestyle, suddenly decided on one spring day in order to forget her, the relationship, overcome the need and the fear, bury the secret and move my life forward. Our dancing had been private. Our tenderness never seen. Our passion caught in a simple smile.

Now I had returned to Paris a year on, having chosen mainstream, unwilling or unequal to risk, or to confront the limits of a society that for a time Cécile and I had negotiated together. When there was nowhere to go to link hands, to dance, to laugh and have fun, like all young lovers, to sit on a bench and be close; forced instead, to choose the sombre streets that led home.

And so, we stood together face-to-face in that kitchen for all those hours. Limbs nestling familiar, our skin warmed, a gentle closing off. How long we stood there I couldn't say. Then, full sunlight, the movement and bustle of morning finally forced us apart...

And my walls, walls that I grew safely within, walls I always thought would be there, the walls that promised and mapped an uncomplicated future, were blasted away, on a night when there was nothing solid or tangible but just two young girls, drawn to each other, who fell in love; and I felt neither loved or fulfilled after the moment, the hours of release; instead, entirely bereft...

walls... and walls and walls... and walls... the destruction of Homs... of its people...

... and the broken walls of Iraq; homes that collapsed, stones that killed and ugly concrete separating tribes and people...

... the southern border of America: division and denigration...

... Hadrian's Wall of fear and protection, and the Berlin Wall of ideological difference, sacrifice, death, martyrdom... separation and broken bonds...

... the breached walls of Jericho.

In those grey hours after that first time, almost two years before, after we slept together in a single bed in a cockroach-infested hostel run by nuns, I felt too weak and sluggish to attempt to wash myself clean. Nothing could cleanse my soul, no soap could ever purge me.

I was confronted instead, with horror and disgust, anticipating a mother's revulsion, society's censure, separation from decency and good living people. My body was now a stranger and no longer mine; this unwanted stranger bearing all that is unclean, corrupt, defining me differently, urging a life I could not live and could not contemplate, denying me an Eternity. The arrival of furtiveness of secrecy and its rooting – and in a very brief moment, any closeness always compromised, distorted, I felt grief over the expected loss of those who loved me, those who trusted me, those who saw me as sensible, sound and clean living. Honesty and straightforwardness had forever taken their leave.

All that was known, relied upon and expected, had been swept away for ever. I was now not who they thought I was, nor was I who I myself had come to know. The walls that safeguarded, kept me within the respectable norms of behaviour had crumbled. Walls that, as I neared caving in, as I looked within myself, as I pleaded and implored those walled supports to please stay upright, fell. The church tower dissolved. The cathedral split down the middle. The Holy Word became a joke; priest and vestments, upbringing, all a travesty. I had become, a lost traveller, an outcast.

Then, a green place without markers, signposts, or well-used pathways, opened up. A new land. And I saw a wall, a wall that I knew I had to climb and I knew that this was the way forward. The wall of survival. And so I climbed, resolutely and continued, edging upwards forever and a lifetime. Uncertain and unstable but always moving upwards, I free climbed, each step precisely placed, choosing with great care and always

Taking charge of one's life involves risk,
because it means confronting a diversity of
open possibilities. (Anthony Giddens, 1991)

with misgivings, wondering always, looking around me, if other routes up might have been better; always wondering if I can.

Over time, other walls that had enclosed and protected me unexpectedly fell. Cascaded down. The bleak spaces left in their wake terrified me, immobilised me, dust blinded and I lost my bearings... like the illness and death of a mother, like the lost words and honesty we didn't ever speak, like the breakdown of a marriage, like a betrayal of someone close, like unfulfilled or faithless friendship, like the failure of a religion, like facing mortality, like realising my own shortcomings and wrongdoings.

And still I climb with hope, sometimes with laughter and a smile, sometimes joyfully, up and over I go. The summits of great and small achievements: finding love, a successful career, a late doctorate, the writing of a book or simply maybe learning another language. Over the years I have gathered some confidence, eventually finding what I can do on this climb, discovering what is too hard. And always that single cushion, that stool for one in a nursery all those years ago, the need for someone to ask, to sit beside me and whisper, 'You are okay because you are being the best that you that you can be.' And because I am free climbing, without ropes or safety harness, I do it alone, contained and thoughtful, assessing, planning, making my own decisions as I go. Climbing on up, resting on the vast ledges of walls which offer refuge, never fully trusting they will hold, always with the urgent need to keep climbing, to find that stone circle, that gathering of ancient walls, those knowledges and wisdoms where I feel I belong and that keep me, where the sun from between the clouds will always pinpoint me, warm me and show me the way.

harmonics

... a harmonic is any member of a harmonic series. The term is employed in various disciplines including in music. It is typically applied to repeating signals based on a fundamental wave and is called the first harmonic; the harmonics which follow are subsequently known as higher harmonics. (Wikipedia)

'never has one seen so many breasts bitten or even chewed in so few pages' wrote an unknown reviewer of Baudelaire's *Les Fleurs du Mal*, when it was first published in 1857. Rémy de Gourmont (1905) described Baudelaire as 'the master par excellence of all the minds... uncorrupted by sentimentalism'. Raynaud said of him in 1917 that through this work he 'restored poetry to its true destiny', that he is as its creator, and arts critic, the father of Impressionism and the founder of Modernism. TS Eliot called him 'the greatest exemplar in modern poetry in any language'.

Baudelaire's poetic masterpiece was hardly greeted with warmth, however, and indeed *Les Bijoux*, along with five others in the collection, was deemed to be an offence to public decency and banned from the first edition of the poetry collection. It was only added much later.

The Jewels (Les Bijoux)

My darling was naked, and knowing my heart well,
She was wearing only her sonorous jewels,
Whose opulent display made her look triumphant
Like Moorish concubines on their fortunate days.

When it dances and flings its lively, mocking sound,
This radiant world of metal and of gems
Transports me with delight; I passionately love
All things in which sound is mingled with light.

She had lain down; and let herself be loved
From the top of the couch she smiled contentedly
Upon my love, deep and gentle as the sea,
Which rose toward her as toward a cliff.

Her eyes fixed upon me, like a tamed tigress,
With a vague, dreamy air she was trying poses...

The additional verse below (translation unattributed, see endnote), written by the poet in his own hand and only discovered very recently, is further evidence of the shocking – for its time – workings of the poet's mind. His genius with words creates images, mesmerising the reader through colour, sound, rhythm and repetition.

Et je fus plein alors de cette Vérité
Que le meilleur trésor que Dieu garde au Génie
Est de connaître à fond la terrestre Beauté
Pour en faire jaillir le Rythme et l'harmonie

And I was full then of this Truth
That the greatest treasure reserved by God for the Genius
Is to know profoundly earthly Beauty
So that from there can spring forth rhythm and harmony

Baudelaire eludes translation writes Jackson (2005). His imagery, like the popular music culture of our times, or Louise Bourgeois' sculpture, the 30 ft high and 33 ft wide spider, *Maman* (1999), is an 'immersive experience'. I spent a very satisfying and intellectually rewarding year rediscovering these verses, exploring, considering and writing poetry in response to 14 of the poems. I wrote with no plan or strategy, simply delving into psychological darkness, for Baudelaire was a dark man, savouring the sublime and the 'putrid' contained in them. These are sexually explicit extravaganzas, firecrackers, outpourings of lust and licence, seductive images of sound and scent, etched like fractured frescos from another era; they are a blurring and blending of colour, pictures painted in soft, fluid words which drip and drift, which move like wisps of smoke, and which led me, as a repressed survivor of the taboos of the '60s and '70s, to uncensored fantasy myself, to places never dreamt or spoken of, to think and write in new, unexpected and unplanned ways.

Once upon a time, on a certain Sunday, I was standing at the mirror wondering what I might wear for family lunch at the home of a colleague of my husband's. I was not relishing the idea, having been somewhat patronised by him on at least one occasion and criticised by others of my husband's legal partnership for returning to my career very soon after the birth of my first child. It was generally held that, as a supportive wife and mother, I should have considered staying at home to make upside-down pineapple cake or master the art of chutney making, with possibly a little charity work for a few hours during the week, something to talk about at coffee mornings, or indeed floral arrangement classes.

In dangerous mood, since his prim, predictable parents were also attending this Sunday lunch, I considered my options. Something demure and sensible, large satin bows maybe, something appropriate for the wife of a West End Edinburgh solicitor. We could, wives together, whip the cream or curl the butter while gossiping about other partners' wives and lovingly tell stories about our head-in-the-clouds husbands. Alternatively, maybe a pair of rebel kitten heels with tight-fitting black and a touch of daredevil sparkle, maybe a bit of voile for a now-you-see them-and-now-you-don't cleavage as I tip forward to hand round the *canapés*. Or again, something to reflect the dirt, sand and grass of travelling the 'flying fox' in the local play park, or chase, catch and roll with my girls, a sort of sweatshirt and designer jeans job... stylish! Certainly, having sown a few seeds of mischief and disruption in the direction of my eldest daughter, who generally on these occasions when duty was required, needed little encouragement, I was more than ready to behave somewhat badly, amidst the ponytails and clean centre partings, the perfect '*Für Elise*' and anorak train sets of their own, polite children.

In the end, I emerged from the bedroom and headed for the car, elegant in black men's tails, that I had picked up for 30 pounds in a closing down sale, my hair gelled flat and glossy, red lipstick and a white silk shirt. The impact was as planned. We were never invited back.

On another occasion, my husband and I had been invited to dinner at the home of one of my own colleagues. I knew that she, old Labour to the core, saw me as able but entirely Tory voting or at best Liberal, and even maybe a little stuck and stodgy. For this occasion, I wore a sleek cream dress, with a low neckline to bring in the boys, sheer, black, seamed tights and black patent heels. Finally, having tried this or that from a random assortment of trinkets and valuables, I topped the outfit with a pink bow tie. This playful nod at cross dressing, which I was on occasion, prone to do, aroused more than a little surprise in what was ultimately a traditional Irish Catholic home.

At some time in the past, maybe through religious legend and parable, the reassuring fantasy of a guardian angel 'ever at my side, who left a home in Heaven to guide, a simple child like me', (words from a 19th century hymn, written by Father Frederick Faber), and the terrors of the all-seeing eye of God, I developed a sense of being always watched, even in private. This placed an inescapable burden of requirement on me. I also started to see life as a constant public performance which I sometimes need to duck by hiding – and when in that mood, crossing the street if I see someone I know, keeping my head down, disappearing with a tent to remote places. I perform, sometimes with great effort, and then I cast off that burden of visibility and seek freedom. However, on the positive side, these contrasts in how I live offer opportunity for superficial identity trialling through creative switching and experimentation in my appearance: taking on aspects of the identity of other people whom I admire or who interest me in some way; a way of dressing, of speaking; creating images for the mirror and the street, for social gatherings, art shows, book events and Michelin restaurants. Change is at the centre of all social phenomena writes Marková (2003) and we change, mutate, alter in response to the impact of 'otherness' on us, often taking to ourselves some aspect of them. This awareness and watchfulness in the company of others, sensing the vibe, has a lot of resonance for how I live my own life. Two questions guide me. What should I wear to look the part? How should an art lover or musician, writer or Board Chair look? As a teacher and in order to look more approachable, to get a bit closer to the source of a child's particular problem, I might wear jeans for example. And secondly, what account do I wish to give of myself? What story do I want to tell? For Italians, the entire jewellery box is in order – all the gold I can muster. For the French, simple, understated face and hair, tending to the girlish; and for the Edinburgh arty middle classes, let's start a riot, wear Doc Martens and speak in the vernacular. In the '90s, I was both privileged and thrilled to see the late Martyn Bennett, a genius of modern Celtic music, enter a community hall in traditional Barra on a Saturday night, wearing pink lace-up boots, tied back hair and a glorious kilt, piping to make your heart pound, like a full Highland cavalcade.

I enjoy clothes, I pore over fashion mags, rake through vintage shops, make lists of what is new, what is edgy; a new lipstick for example, Topshop skinny denim, or a recycled '60s kipper tie. I can still feel dizzy at a new fabric or a cut of trousers never seen before, rushing out of the changing room lest utterly overcome with excitement, I should pass out: a T-shirt in rubber say, a well-tailored, laminated, or gold PVC skirt, or an in-your-face green. Each one, a new me. But while I have cross-dressed for impact or fun, I have never wanted to be other than a woman. I enjoy being a woman in every aspect, and that includes childbirth, for which I felt I had been destined (though I had had no inkling of this prior to the event) and physically engineered for the 'production line'. In giving birth and at that supremely defining moment, when you are only physical, your mind and impulses all one, when the world around you has faded to no longer being, I felt I had finally grasped and understood the entirety of my body, the nature and immense power of it, its primeval origins, connectedness to the beat and turning of things universal, a power much greater, grander and more forceful than me. As in death I guess, in childbirth your mind and will are no match for the primitive, natural forces that drive it and your body will do what it must, follow its genetic destiny and take you into history.

Impermanence and changeability, continual possibility and movement, adventure, curiosity and self-making at every turn; responsiveness and improvised selfdom dependant on where, what and who; variability and flow; each and all define my existence. I am a sexually fluid woman of fixed gender, open to the totality of a person rather than their gender. It is who they are that draws me. Both what might be termed the feminine and the masculine in others produce different selves and different presentations and behaviours in me. I have done hair bows and hair bands, backless, shoulderless and braless, gold chain anklets and garters, leather, fox furs and suspenders. These are mere trinkets for the nursery, props for play and playacting. I have also worn cufflinks, arm cuffs, ties, and waistcoats to work; top hats and deerstalkers to eat lunch with friends in town. I have done lumberjack, hip hop and grandad, Bobby Sox and army sweats. I have scoured the vintage shops of Edinburgh for a man's tuxedo, for shirts and cravats. There is only fun to be had in this mix: masculine with the showgirl, cabaret and girly crush; clinging black lace with boy jeans or stiff boxy tailoring. Builder's boots with a Fairy Queen skirt was not so commonplace in the '80s as it currently is. In not conforming to how a woman is expected to dress, act, react, express herself sexually, as women today, we can and should challenge perceptions, expectations and the stereotypes of gender from the past.

Second wave feminism and thought in the '60s which lasted for two decades, brought a flurry of writing on sexuality, women in the workplace and female reproductive rights. Anne Dickson's *The Mirror Within* brought to the conversation long overdue attention to the female body, orgasm, masturbation and body image. This work, and many similar books of its time, has helped and paved the way for increasing openness and honesty about being female. Only very recently, and not before time, sanitary products are finally free and available in UK schools and places of education in order to counter period poverty. My youngest daughter has no coyness at work with regard to a heavy menstrual flow. Rather than concocting a euphemism, if it creates practical problems she states it plainly. Dickson's book was a beacon for those of us who still remember the shame associated with sanitary pads, the way they were wrapped in brown paper bags and handed covertly to our mothers over the counter of the chemist shop.

Not long ago, I bought Marge Piercy's novel, *Woman on the Edge of Time,* published in 1976, but which I read ten years later, as required background reading for my three fiercely feminist daughters. They were not impressed at this futurist vision written nearly 25 years ago, disappointingly but when I thought about it, understandable. The issues of phallocentrism and patriarchal models of society, of threats to the environment, of cultural primacy and ethnocentrism, of consumerism, imperialism and class subordination to list just a few, are no longer conversations to be had about an imagined future. These are discourses of the present moment, the stuff of our daily Google digests, on Facebook and other social media.

The actions of Greta Thunberg and those of all the young protesters are outstanding examples, supported by popular movements across the globe; Tarana Burke's initiative in 2006 and the powerful #MeToo revelations have exposed behaviour that exploited women for decades, provided a powerful voice for those affected and brought down some of the most powerful and successful men of our generation. Recycled clothes have hit the catwalks, vintage is the hallmark of responsible buying; the status of migrants is the stuff of government debate across the globe, the democratic will, political vested interests and ideology; and while politicians erect monuments to capitalism, feed multi-national corporations in order to reward these already privileged, charities and community activists provide the much needed remedial work of care and material help in an attempt to right the imbalance. For any socially aware young person or millennial, Piercy's book says nothing new. Certainly, the global swing away from liberalism is alarming. Anti-abortion activists are gaining some ground in parts of the USA and women's rights have no chance of being protected never mind progressed under this ruthless and frightening Presidency. Daily struggles concerning status, rights, power, dignity and equality still continue within families, the workplace, and in the social and private sphere. Sex reassignment surgery is indeed available throughout all European states though the legal age at which a child can request this continues to vary, and experts remain divided on matters of gender identity – to what extent gender, social interaction and associated behaviours are a social construct. Nonetheless, there has been progress.

Some sociologists like Giddens for example, rightly argue that within contemporary society tradition has lost its power and people have a greater ability to be 'reflexive' or to consider how they respond to their social world; we have a free choice as to how we act and who we want to be. As traditions wane, the individual becomes the new centre of agency and responsibility and we can no longer rely on set ways of living our lives. We are solely responsible for our existence. Repressive social structures and norms that perpetuate expectations are certainly being challenged everywhere we look. Those rituals and social practices around partnering, parenting, pregnancy and insemination, as well as social hierarchies and behaviours in the workplace and at social gatherings, in job recruitment, even in political arenas have changed substantially. What becomes clear is that we can no longer assume anything. It is commonplace to declare a partnership after three dates; an appropriate app, akin to an Uber treat delivered to your phone, your bed or your door, will find you a sex partner nearby in minutes or sperm of your choice to create a baby.

There is much evidence to support gender fluidity and a growing body of research within the social sciences, psychology, in medicine and science, in addition to the personal testimony of individuals, to support that reality. Gender fluidity, mixed gender is not a new phenomenon. In ancient times 'two spirit people', a term used by indigenous North Americans to describe mixed gender individuals who were blessed with both a masculine and a feminine spirit, were greatly valued by their tribes as possessing special and unique spiritual gifts.

The Enlightenment of this century must surely be the uncoupling of sexual behaviour and reproductive practice, encouraging us to see sexual activity in a totally different way. Despite the best efforts of the wedding industry and saccharine press, gender, as is increasingly understood and accepted, is not consistent. In the same way as every individual constructs identities in response to mainly external factors and our identity is never fixed but open, we can argue that gender is also a construct, rooted less in biological and hormonal factors and much more enacted as a response to societal factors.

Gender is performed and is as variable, complex and contradictory as the identities that we build for ourselves. I very much welcome the current trend towards a non-binary society, and the creation or a safe space for gender-neutral individuals. I see these developments as a stage in humankind's evolutionary journey. Freedom for people and society as a whole to self-identify in relation

What clearly emerges is that whatever we mean when we talk about gender – whether it is biological sex, a socially constructed role we perform, a personal identity or a combination of all three, it is fluid. (Hines, 2018)

to gender, to define themselves in whatever way, is liberating and opens the way to the development of radically different individual behaviour, appearance, vocabulary and language. And a complete reinvention of society.

I have long waited for the world to catch up with the reality of nuanced sexuality and fluid gender and of the freedom to speak them, live them without fear of criticism or prejudice. Sexual and gender identities are too important to deny. I have lived through a time of stereotyping and censure, of fear and rebuttal. The shifting identities that we take on, enact or incarnate are central to our happiness and fulfilment and critical to societal health. I would never have had the courage to break an existing mould or to challenge taboos in the way that today's brave pioneers have done: Virginia Prince (1912–2009), for example, who was born a man but from an early age preferred to present as a woman. In establishing the magazine *Transvestia* she made a significant contribution to the public's awareness of trans-people and popularised the word 'transgender'. Many entertainers such as Sam Smith, Phillip Schofield, David Walliams, Jonathan Van Ness from *Queer Eye* and countless sports personalities have all declared themselves to be LGBTQ. And like many, I am grateful that I can now be absolutely who I am.

I am not an expert on gender or on evolutionary theory, nor would I wish to enter debates on biological essentialism or trans rights within the feminist movement but I am persuaded by experts who forecast evolutionary change, whose predictions point to the emergence of superhumans either by genetic modification or cybernetic implants. In 2018 Stephen Hawkings wrote:

> during this century, people will discover how to modify both intelligence and instincts such as aggression... some people won't be able to resist the temptation to improve human characteristics, such as memory, resistance to disease and length of life... once such superhumans appear, there will be significant political problems with unimproved humans, who won't be able to compete... presumably, they will die out, or become unimportant. Instead, there will be a race of self-designing beings who are improving at an ever-increasing rate.

Futurist writers too, such as Piercy and her predictions in the '70s, have not been so far from the mark and Ursula Le Guin's *The Left Hand of Darkness* challenges depictions of race and gender in her portrayal of a society where women and men all share the same biological and emotional make-up. The interchangeability of certain species and their roles, and sexual fluidity in others, are well documented. The male emu nests with its egg, incubates and nurtures its young. During the mating process of sea horses the female deposits her eggs on the male's tail, which he then carries until they hatch. Certain species of fish such as the kobudai may reproduce as a female in the first part of life, but breed as a male in the second part thus doubling its reproductive output. Other species continually mutate according to circumstances and to the need for survival. Some transform gender and ability to mate in order to fill a vacuum. We know that the evolutionary process is one of adaptation, of genetic variation in response to societal and environmental change.

Given these and other major indicators, increasing scientific and medical advances that we see every day, mutations and changes that we take for granted, I believe that as a species, in a constantly changing environment, in order to survive, post-apocalypse, pandemic or whatever, we are currently on an evolutionary journey. We are in transition towards a higher or new state of existence. From the debris of extinction of many species, including our own, other species will emerge: 'The defining characteristic of humanity is not the hardware within but the relationships between persons... how the mind and body will evolve in response to cultural definitions of gender' (Bolger, 2006). These are key questions for the future of the species.

Most importantly, what future there is for humankind aside, I believe that the human race is much greater intellectually and physically than we know, I am convinced that the social meanings of what it means to be a man or a woman are not yet settled and 'we tell histories about what it meant to be a woman at a certain time and place... we track the transformation of those categories over time' (Butler; New Statesman, September, 2020) for now, I invite people of all ages to be honest and bold, to consider from an open position, another destiny, who they are in essence, irrespective of

*We may be fast approaching a new
singularity, when all the concepts that
give meaning to our world – me, you,
men, women, love and hate – will become
irrelevant. (Yuval Noah Harari)*

social constructs, what they really want and what excites
them, what approaches and roles in sexual partnerships
satisfy them and their sex partner best. There may be
possibility and potential unrealised. We know from
the experts on sexual behaviours, that women's sexual
orientation may vary throughout a lifetime.

A society that celebrates that variability is indeed
one to aspire to. A real coming to grips with gender
and sexual identity is central to who we are and the
process of self-realisation and self-making is a vital one.

We cannot underestimate the role of sexual energy,
curiosity and interest in making us brim with life and
joy, bright with curiosity and a keen appetite for the
adventure of each new day. As I understand sexual
behaviour and procreation generally, it seems to me that
the role of women in societal change is pivotal. In this
passing and volatile phase of history that we currently
inhabit as women, however we define and enact our
own gender, our current contribution to human
development I believe, is to counter toxic masculinity
where we see it, to take up space, to be assertive when
necessary, reserve tenderness and softness, oodles of
oxytocin for our most intimate relationships and then,
let it all gush, spurt and flow. Now more than ever, it is
our time, in the rising waves of questions, redefinition
and reassignment, to respond, as both younger and

importantly not so young 'invisible' women, to come forth from whatever cultural tomb has been created for us or we have created for ourselves; to emerge strong, resolute and clear about who we are and to stand firmly on the same ground, in the same sun, sleep under the same moon as men. And I exhort women and men today for the tomorrow of your children, to mother and to father our sons and daughters equally – without favour, expectation, imposition, interference or difference – not to 'groom' or shape but rather to enable and promote gender freedom: to create an expectation in fresh, new generations that they will 'live freely, without fear, discrimination or violence against the genders that they are' (Butler, 2020).

Note

'Les Bijoux', originally appeared in the second (1861) edition of Charles Baudelaire's *Les Fleurs du Mal*.

The translation (1954) of the first excerpt given in this essay is by William Aggeler.

A previously unknown verse was unveiled when a book containing it, handwritten by the author, appeared at auction in November 2019: amp.theguardian.com/books/2019/nov/14/baudelaires-erotic-poem-revealed-the-jewels-les-fleurs-du-mal

runner

... the icy air cuts like a blade. Snow cracks and splinters under my Nike Pegasus shoes and I have just reached the top of the road to Bonaly Hill. My body is well warmed with the effort, snug in waterproofs. It's a silent Sunday of church and late sleeping. With the sun on my chilled skin, the sky brightly blue, I go from a trudging jog to a steady run and my heart fills with the glorious sight of Edinburgh's jagged skyline and the cold blue of the Firth of Forth beyond. My heart rate has slowed to a steady rhythm which powers me along. My breath clouds around my face. This kind of joy is hard to describe. I seek it again and again and I have found it, over and over, for almost 25 years.

There have been many small but memorable victories. Shaving a minute off the time of my usual four mile run. The triumphant and very public mile or two on the final straight to the finish line of a half marathon and even better, a full-blown 26.2 mile marathon. Breaking through the heaviness of my legs, dissolving lead, achieving the physical ease that make my feet light as I run on air. I remember that night of snowfall and severe weather warnings. We drew curtains, lit a fire, made plans for no school in the morning either for me – I was a teacher then – or my three girls. I cooked a meal for the family. Later, the television switched on, everyone 'cooried in' and I slipped out of the door, over the threshold, in trepidation and excitement both. I wanted to catch the night, hold it in my hands, breathe it in, be in and of it. The dead white wilderness of the residential street, dotted with imperious lampposts, took my mind and swallowed me so completely that I was suddenly, somehow, whole. My world. Where I should be. Where no one else was or had ever been. All for me, as I broke the snow's crust under my feet and marked this new world with my footsteps.

I started jogging in my 30s. After several warnings from my doctor about deteriorating lung capacity, following numerous bouts of bronchitis, and an inability to reach the top of a stair without feeling breathless, I stopped smoking. It wasn't gradual, that hadn't worked before. It was hardcore. I had been smoking around 30 cigarettes a day, maybe more. Nicotine curling, creeping and fizzing in every blood vessel had been a delight. But then, after a few cigarette-free days, maybe it was weeks, I found that I had more oxygen than I felt my body could manage. It was as if I was aerated; and I became aware of a new restlessness which I must satisfy or overcome.

There were times when I felt I was a gas balloon about to explode in mid-air. Though I had played squash throughout my 20s, no doubt attracted by the image, the sports club, smart glass and chrome courts, winged feet (a female Hermes indeed), a neat racket, white Aertex shirts, hot showers and a fresh orange and tonic with Morgan and Mercedes owners afterwards, I have no recollection of why I took to running.

My first effort lasted all of 15 minutes, though only

two or three of those consisted of what could be called 'running'. Mainly, I walked, in drizzle, among dogs, on the dreary expanse of the Meadows in Edinburgh's Tollcross. The first few outings were unpleasant, my clumsiness and unease very public. My body felt stiff and ungainly and the feeling that there was no breath left was unnerving. Then I discovered a surprising confidence. There were always some more breaths I could take. It was just a question of going beyond what I had considered to be my limitations.

Getting used to launching myself beyond what seemed like a threshold, stepping boldly on to unknown terrain, pushing against all the resistances of lungs and limbs, and the boundaries in my mind, this paradigm of who I was, was a challenge; but somehow exciting. I was becoming someone else. I could be someone else. In rising to both the challenge of relinquishing a damaging addiction and undertaking an activity which was far from anything I had ever dreamed of, during those runs, I had altered completely. I was beginning to see myself as not only a runner but a winner. I could see possibility, grasped it, wrestled it into being. Clad in my running shoes with ample toeboxes and anti-pronation support, a Pertex vest, technologically designed to 'wick away' sweat, sunshine, and rain brought wonder, frolics and joy in equal measure. Most of all they brought renewal.

Running became my private space to build and refresh. In an overcrowded life it offered everything that meditation or prayer could provide. I found mindspace on those four-mile half hours and those longer Sunday six milers through the green peace of Colinton Dell. Fresh, healing leafiness, the joy of mud, the thrill of a soaking, rain running down my face, sloshing through puddles, represented such retreat, as fulfilling and bountiful for me as a week in a convent, a vow of silence and monastic contemplation. Never had I had such fun. Never had I been so loose, so carefree and silly; indeed downright hysterical. Never had I had the joy of total aloneness. I laughed at the downpours, smiled up at the clouds and sunshine, and spoke wild words to pavements and pathways, flowers and canals. And when the hills slowed me, I cursed them repeatedly and venomously or sang 'You Are My Sunshine' loudly until I reached the top. Upon which I threw my arms up in triumph shouting, 'Got you, you bastard!'

I was not built for running of course. I was too heavy and too flat footed – my feet are too big and clumsy – they have always been much slower than my body to respond. I am a good dancer in that I move well, at my best when I am suggestive, my hips afloat, shoulders in orbit and more or less rooted to the same spot. (I am for many reasons ashamed to admit that the idea of dancing in a cage surrounded by a bar filled with people, as was the attraction in one Edinburgh pub in the '70s, rather appealed.)

Physical activity classes at school represented horrors for me. Sessions on a hockey pitch involved chasing a girl I had been instructed to 'mark' for no reason that I could fathom, since neither she nor I ever had possession of that lethal missile of a hockey ball nor indeed wanted it. Rather like trigonometry, the purpose of position, structure and layout on the hockey pitch was unclear. I managed to duck the hockey, not the maths sadly, by having a period or asthma, or needing time to practise piano for a grade exam. My luck was in if all three factors presented at the same time. I was better on the netball court where my height served me well as a 'shoot' but running for the ball was never part of that success. I just caught it and threw it upwards. In the gym hall, I was a disaster, clinging like a dead weight to a wooden beam or dully suspended from a thick rope, immobile, hands raw and burnt by the friction of any movement including the slow slide downwards, waiting for the light and limber to complete their own superior journeys up and down or across the room.

Jumping over the horse was even worse although I did in fact master the technique of leaping, hands centred on the leather structure and between my legs, which were spread wide and high. I had full faith that my teacher, would catch me on the other side but whenever she did, I virtually knocked her down as she staggered backwards muttering in recovery, 'Oh Anne, what a weight!'

When I started running in my early 30s I saw it as a means of overcoming a habit and of controlling weight. And when the need for cigarettes eventually departed, I cannot say that I became slimmer, only fitter and more solid. I was probably never a joy to observe. At times I attracted some unpleasant attention, mainly from men in vans, or startled cats even, but I progressed in five minute increments, each time increase a matter for celebration, until I could sustain a 20 minute aerobic session without stopping.

I remember clearly my first experience of a 'second wind'. I was running in the noble and fragrant Grange area of Edinburgh. I was flagging, considering cutting short, when my energy level suddenly picked up and I felt I could run forever. Excited, I had read of such events, it was a kind of runner's Enlightenment. I finished at my doorstep in a state of near-hysterical jubilation. Not only had I managed to reduce my time per mile, I was now beginning to have an authentic runner's experience. Such milestones led me eventually to my first half marathon. It was in Glenrothes. I sent off my application in a moment of thoughtlessness and over-exuberance. My number and instructions came by post and I left them aside for me to ponder at leisure.

When the day arrived, I remember lying in bed, knowing a decision had to be made. Much easier to let it go, have a quiet run and relax into the day with my family. Then in a sudden burst of determination and anti-defeatism, despite the nerves in my stomach and uncertainty about how it would be: would I come in last? Would I find the start line? Was my gear passable? Might I take ill and require medical assistance? I gathered my things, left a sleeping household and drove to Fife. It was a breakthrough and the first of many half marathons (often six or eight a year), 10K and 5K events.

In April 1991, at the age of 42, I ran the London Marathon, that trophy event for all runners. I didn't stop. I ran every mile, with cramp at the end, but in glory! I still have the blessed shoes with which I crossed that finish line. I competed in the Great North Run and an 18 mile race in Glasgow; I collected all the renowned 'must do' running events, travelling as far as Dundee, where I had the honour of running in the same crowd as an over 70 year old personality called Jenny who always wore a cotton hat, ran marathons up and down the country in her own time and was renowned for her pluck; and in Liverpool and Newcastle too.

Running was from start to finish a lone pursuit.

I had no wish to become a member of a group or to join a fun run with friends. The journey was mine, a challenging but fulfilling relationship between me and the miles. If I had any problems that worried me – muscle spasm, nausea after exertion, unexpected bowel movements, a tight calf, aching Achilles tendon, I turned only to a good physiotherapist. I researched, chose and collected my gurus. Books or magazines on training to run were more interesting than reading about the lives of famous runners. On the few occasions that I did run with someone else, the sociability of it, the presence of someone else changed my experience, reduced it to chatter and took away from its true essence and purpose.

For many people running is a sport, a competition with oneself or with others. Like many activities which become part of our lives, we participate for different reasons. My motive was to remedy an unhealthy lifestyle. To my surprise, it revealed much more. Running became a means of remaking myself, a way of stopping and of refocusing.

A long run could be many things, a theological or philosophical exploration or reconciliation of ideas, a formulation of schemes and plans both major and trivial, a soothing massage, a calming curative. A replaying in my head of something joyful, an affirming or promising encounter, an energising conversation; a thrilling piece of music. It could result in a decision to delve, to reorientate or travel in new directions. Short routine runs were for the purpose of shedding, using up unspent energy and preparing my mind for a forthcoming demand. Runs of an hour or more were neutral spaces which I could fill and colour at will. During these gifts of unscheduled time, I could meditate, see the world as I passed through, but it was as if incidental to my mental state of interrogation, deep attachment; or else non-attachment to what is clear, empty and not solid and a sense of floating through what is tangible and concrete.

In sharing this important, life-enhancing experience of mine, my purpose is to convey a more general message. Like any activity there are often key implications for self-discovery and self-creation: the ordinary and commonplace can lead to fundamental shift, if we are willing, open, flexible and accepting. We adhere to the world by dwelling in the familiar most certainly, but we grow in worlds where we are a stranger, where we are uncomfortable. A pomegranate is composed mainly of seeds, a multiplicity contained by fibres. But seeds fly. They are blown in different directions by the wind. They are carried. They migrate, cross new frontiers, grow and root. In flight they are subject to chaos.

It is this randomness, this effect of change and variability, this continual movement that is the essence of living a life. While rooting and abiding is comfortable, it is our confrontation with the unrehearsed, the puzzling, the unsettling, the unprepared for, that makes us grow and keeps the spiders at bay. Running exposed a self, a potential for well-being, intense joy and wonder that I did not know existed within me. It taught me about our connection with grass, wind and snow; the complexity of being human, the multi-faceted nature of who we are, the possibilities of being, in so many different ways and at different levels. I found a truer, more solid self through running. I am the person who together with an obsession with clothes and fashion, likes mud, dirty legs, a runny nose and rain pouring down my face. In short, I like looking grubby. Nothing in my life history suggested any of these things. But I had reached a critical point when I had to do something radical, even if it involved putting myself in a position of looking absurd, feeling inadequate and undertaking something I was ill-equipped for and knew nothing about. The outcome of that wonderful adventure of fellow-runners, well-wishers, of woodland, hills and beaches, of constantly trying and giving it all you've got, enhanced many years of my life.

The smell of Germolene is evocative. I had to give up running ten years ago because of the wear and tear on my limbs. I still dream of maybe trying just a few steps when the day is just the kind of day that invites you to run. That unique aroma brings back the nerves, struggle and sheer exhilaration of the race. And although I was always a lone runner at these events, there were occasions when I was utterly grateful for a kind word: 'No long now hen' from a gruff Fifer or a group of supportive women as I turned the corner of a street in Aberfeldy. In Dundee at mile ten, with three more to go, I lost pace and energy. A sturdy man was suddenly at my side. 'Come on' he said, 'I'll run with you,' and so he did. Together we entered the stadium, supporters all around clapping and at the finish line, 'Anne Pia from Edinburgh' on the loudspeaker, and my proud mum, my husband and girls smiling broadly.

on miracles

... there is no God and this was not how it was meant to be. There had been such expectation around. Such buoyancy and good will. It had gone so well. For a first time, it had been a pretty good effort. I had even taken a moment to put on a bit of lipstick before coming through the swing doors to re-enter the world. And here I was now, alone in the half light, at 2.00am, perched on a stool, only room for one and how I wanted the warm presence of someone else to sit beside me, someone to tell me it would all be okay... that God would see us through. I was 31, had always thought you see, that someone somewhere made sure you would be safe, that answers would come. That nothing was for life... that things usually ended well.

I don't know what's happening but Paul is outside in the corridor leaning against the wall... he is yellow in the face... she has taken it very badly... such a shame...

... please, please listen to me... my bonding with my baby is not in question... I just need someone to help me cope... please stop observing me as if I am wanting in some way... can someone please help us... tell us what is going to happen...

… we need somewhere where we can really, really cry and howl and hold each other… can you give us a private space?

… please God make this go away… I am pleading for a miracle… please give her my legs, take it all, but make her whole…

In the nursery, shivering with shock in my nightclothes, shadows moving in, out, around me, voices low, concerns only about latching on, nipples and milk production, about my emotional capacity to take to my child as my own, I was feeding my little girl whose little legs were not even. Nothing more and nothing less. Less would have been wonderful. How far would more stretch? How much would it require of us?

But there was no knowledgeable doctor, no expert, to smile and reassure. Just this damned focus on the mechanics of waking, feeding, winding and 'instinctive' mothering. Just this absence of words.

Just get on with the job. Be pragmatic. We won't talk about the dropping heaviness in your gut, your inability to swallow, the thudding in your head, the dopey confusion and blurring of all my senses, the dozing rather than restful sleep.

I was lost, shipwrecked… powerless to find any intellectual way forward, around the solid, uncompromising reality which seemed to block my ability to think or even feel, without anything spiritual or shred of religious belief to hold on to that would make this bearable, that would make anything better. Except that she was utterly, with her black hair and blue wondering eyes, absolutely beautiful. And as I looked at her, there was such a wobbling in my throat, such a tremor in my hands as I saw in my mind, my little girl, full of play, limping across the grass, trying to stay upright on legs that could not hold her; joyfully and laughingly, unaware of any limitation, while others stared at her impediment.

And I knew in that moment that there was no God and that I had been invoking emptiness then and throughout my life. Up to that point, I had been a devout Catholic.

And I knew that we, all three of us, my husband, my daughter and I, faced something individually and together, that was unfathomable, unending. This was a task, an undertaking in which we stood alone: afraid and insecure, as for the many years that followed, we knocked on every medical door up and down the UK, followed every lead both here and abroad, in an attempt to find some ground-breaking specialist that had the gift of miracles; and unsupported, as we confronted the reactions and prejudices, the cruelties of a society and the world around us on a daily basis. That need to suddenly assume a lifetime of responsibility since there were no answers, to seek out the best in orthopaedics; and the need also to self-defend, to protect and to teach our growing girl resilience against insulting behaviour and words, would consume us, possess us and alter everything that we understood about life and destiny and strength of character.

This was an event that fundamentally altered forever, our view of our fellow human beings.

We saw something we had not suspected or seen before.

We learned to trust less; to still hope but expect little.

... these things bring families together... it is God's will and a gift... you are blessed... fuck off... I can see that she does not need my blessing or counsel... this is a comfortable home with plenty support... but we will pray in the parish... we haven't seen you at Mass for a while... and you won't again... can I talk about it... please let me talk about it... please don't change the subject... look me in the eye...

... there are support groups, people with children who have similar problems... Thalidomide... Achondroplasia... I'll send you some details

... no, no... I don't want to be part of their club... we will not take on a disablist frame of mind... we will not wallow... I don't want to meet them...

Just before visiting hour, three or four days after my baby was born, a paediatrician came into the nursery where I was quietly feeding her. We were told about the absence of a fully formed hip joint and missing or shortened bones in one leg, that the cause was unknown and the medical strategy confused and not simple.

... Oh was it the games of squash and the partying when I didn't know you were there, my lovely girl?... what was it that I did that halted the blood supply to your leg for that split second? Is it genetic? Is it my fault? Are we being punished for something that I did? Have I burdened you through whatever I did or didn't do as I carried you, with a lifetime of difficulties; and that you and any future children we and later you might have, might be similarly affected...

... si, si Dio esiste... ma un dio cattivo... maybe that's how it is... an evil god... betrayed, betrayed...

Hardly able to stand, never mind walk, with my husband and mother close behind, I entered the ward and smiling, for I now at this moment, had to be two people, I warmly greeted our excited visitors. It was a question of finding and saying the words. It was a question of reaching an equilibrium and control where the necessary information could be communicated while the emotions – fear, sadness, indignation, such tenderness and pain for a small innocent, my precious flesh and blood, for she grew inside my body (her body was part of mine) could be contained, and would not flood out in an endless stream that would overthrow us, suffocate us and would start me crying and never, ever stop.

But no, this was not how we wanted the world to greet her. We wanted to glory in all the flowers, the cards and endless gifts – at the mere fact of her. We wanted to engage with the greater event, not with her disability, but with her glorious arrival, her undoubted wonderful nature and character, her potential in life and what she would add to ours. We wanted to engage with her strength and not disable her, not make her impotent by focusing on her vulnerability.

While the 14 years of operations, of bone grafting and leg lengthening would be the dark shadow skulking in the margins of all that we did as a family, we only acknowledged and summoned it when it was necessary, when there was no escape and when only days remained before another consultation or more surgery.

For two weeks, Paul, my mother and I kept our secret. The world believed all to be well. This was a triumph of double dealing and deception. Then slowly, to my husband's family first and then my own, we told the story. We told it so well, we acted our chosen roles so convincingly in fact, that I think to this day, no one apart from my husband, my children and my mother, realised the emotional energy, the tears, highs and lows of every operation, of every recovery and every new step as our toddler, then our child at school, then our teenager, took, as she learned to walk again and again and again and as she began to realise herself, and we witnessed her own fear, her own coming to terms with yet more surgery, more pain and what the mirror told her. Her confrontation with a world that would only alienate. Not one saw our anger at the questions and gratuitous comments from passers-by in the supermarket or in some pizzeria. Not one saw the nights in post-operative wards, as our baby cried out when they turned her, cleaned her wounds after surgery and I tried to soothe, and later to clean every wound myself.

... I want to stay with her... she is 18 months old and she is going to theatre tomorrow... I'm sorry but there are no beds for you... that's fine, I'll just sit here all night...

Thank you to the wonderful dark-haired angel, who came on night duty, found a side ward and against all the rules, put us both in there where we could try to sleep... where I lay beside my daughter and held her all night.

... yes, I'm the hospital social worker... you know that you are not making this any easier for yourselves... it's unreasonable to expect me to go and leave my baby... I'm afraid those are the rules, no parents after hours... well I am staying anyway and you will not move me...

... is that you Mrs Pia... I'm just phoning to say that it may be that we cannot accommodate your daughter's needs any longer at this school unless you consider spending the day yourself with her here as she moves from classroom to classroom...

... Mum, I have tickets for the gig in Manchester... Take That... no one at school wants to come with me... I heard them talking about it in the room next door... will you come...

... and in this case, we would of course, recommend amputation... my husband has fainted... you will find if you don't wish to take this decision, that you are embarking on a very hard road indeed and I am not sure if we will be successful...

My daughter was seven years old, and I thought of her in bed with a lover... one leg missing; I thought of her fumbling for her prosthesis as she stumbled around the bedroom at night trying to get to the toilet... I thought of an empty trouser leg and I thought of how she would feel about her body. And our answer was no. We will take this harder road and we will take our chances.

We, my husband, mother and I, and my daughter

included, tried so hard, performed so well, covered our hearts and expressions so expertly, sometimes even to each other... summoned interests, laughter and a love of fun so artfully, that we made it all seem so easy. And so... not that we wanted sympathy... but understanding about cancelled arrangements, forgotten birthdays, sudden changes of plan; concern even from those close to us was sparse. And from the corporate world that my husband inhabited, completely absent. In fact they added to the pressure.

Our happy place was an eatery in Sheffield called Hanrahans. Discharged from Hallam Children's Hospital, where they called me 'duck' and teased me for arriving late in the morning, where the first sign of Christmas made me cry, and where I brought in takeaways of everything that my post-op daughter might fancy, we feasted in Hanrahans as a family. We ate everything we liked the look of and we laughed and cried with relief at the thought of going home. It was in that cool place in our usual corner where a wheelchair could fit that we discovered Mexican treats and wonderful chips.

I don't think I have ever since experienced a joy quite like that of getting home. Home took on a completely different meaning then. Yes, undoubtedly, home where, days after another major operation... to stabilise her hip with bone grafting, inserting pins into a surgically broken leg in the hope that growth in both tibia and femur would take place to bring length, a box arrived from the orthopaedic workshop with yet another newly raised shoe; made to different specifications; and yes, to be honest, the new looked not a great deal different from the pre-op versions. And we would not cry or speak our dismay to each other she and I, but instead still speak about maybes. She did protest loudly, and who wouldn't, at my cack-handed nursing skills, yelling her disapproval... appealing for a more tender approach.

But more importantly, our home, our pleasure-filled oasis, became a place of bustle, noise, light and laughter. It was our shout out after the grimness of the hospital ward and the indeterminate x-rays. It was a place where the next consultation and medical possibilities, disappointments and anxieties were put aside while we threw ourselves into ordinary and normal... our three girls' banter as they, each sister, rediscovered their old ways with each other; our kitchen a warm, abundant place of plenty and too much; where wine flowed and friends came. Home where months later she, herself, having recovered from operation after operation, whizzed around the neighbourhood, one leg in the air on her BMX bike, threatening the health of the indigenous trees that had served the locality well for centuries; used her crutch as a weapon; climbed the walls between nearby houses; fell off walls. Our home was where she nurtured her impressive mind and musicality and became an avid reader of everything and anything well beyond her years... an accomplished pianist and violinist, and whatever instrument she put her hand to; where she brought her school prizes, her friends and some years later, I have no doubt, her lovers. The ramp for her wheelchair when not put to its intended use, was used as a booby trap for naive childminders and unsuspecting visitors. And, persuaded mainly by her, rather than by the two younger girls, to roller blade down it, our cleaner (overnight turned carer) near broke her neck as she hurtled down the slope and landed headfirst in our bushes. My growing daughter took everything in. From the *Friends, Eastenders, Coronation Street, Mrs Doubtfire and The Sound of Music*, TV presentations to the antics of Take That, Michael Jackson and her own mother.

... I'm running in the school sports... I don't think that's a good idea... if you want to... it will be hard you know... I'm going to... I think you should go and get your little girl... she is still running around the track and the race has finished...

She is now a woman and parent herself. I could say that we have learned to live with what life determined for us. I think it would be more accurate to say that all the emotions that we reacted with to every twist and turn of those years of operations are still alive, but while easily aroused as they are now (as I write the story for the first time), they mostly lie buried under the changing circumstances and scenarios of our existence. Her physical disability is something she copes with still, from the time she gets out of bed, takes the tube, walks in the streets to work or some art gallery, sits around a meeting table, and slips into the night life of popular music, gigs and the occasional photoshoots with the idols of the music scene, glamorous St Vincent, Sleater-Kinney and the like, that is part of her work. The disability is her every day.

Sometimes she is laughed at, whispered about or a finger is pointed in her direction. She is often too, it must be happily acknowledged, Customer of the Day at her usual breakfast stop, which earns her her morning coffee. It never gets any easier.

Nonetheless she has come to be more often than not, greater, more powerful, stronger in mind and constitution than these occurrences, wounding as they are.

Stronger than the traction/pulley device that she spent the first year of her life in, her leg suspended above her which limited any cuddling, jiggling or calming skin-to-skin contact.

Stronger than the frog splint that contained and made her rigid from the chest down for months. Stronger than the plaster and improvised trolley that she lay on after each operation which allowed us to take her out with us, and which we pulled along behind us as we trailed through the supermarket for the weekly food shopping or treated ourselves in a Burger King

Stronger than the crutches and ironmongery of fixators that we all endured, couldn't look too closely at, explained away to her sisters, dispelled the horror and treated as a normal device to make her better. Yes, she eventually towered above them, above these grotesque contraptions that in honesty cracked me up, opened up in me deep chasms of dark despair and insecurity about what if anything can we rely on, as I repeatedly and I have no doubt she did too, asked the great gods of the sky and universe and every living creature,

'Why? Why? Why?'

And within the limits imposed by her often dreadful situation, she resolutely drew from some wellspring within her, for the expert role she now holds in London in a world famous corporation and a purposeful and full life.

... in time we will replace your hip... and we could of course amputate your leg...

My daughter gradually gained the wings of excellence and endurance – of trust as well. When I look at the woman she is, the layers of adulthood and maturity fall away and I see through to the loving, fragile child in her with so much to give and so much to glory in. She has grown to be a good, good person; well-loved for her charisma, wit, mind and mischief. In her wake I have learned a lot. Mostly I learned humility and was stripped of my precious elitism. Our elegant Alfetta sports car and the middle class paraphernalia of social contact didn't quite seem to matter anymore; to hell with the dinner parties, the small talk and the garden Escallonia; to hell too with the badges, the hierarchies and the pomposities; the exclusionary language and practices. The stuff of life is how we react, confront and find ways to deal with what we didn't want or expect, how we recover ourselves, stay steady through what shatters, terrifies and cuts us down.

Travelling those years with her, I too learned lessons that deeply affected and dictated the direction of my own professional life working on behalf of socially disadvantaged children and people in education, lessons that I preached from the heart and the head ever after. The world is not just for winners; not just for the privileged, those born to ready stardom. The challenge is to encourage and cultivate stardom in those around us, to hear diverse voices, to mainstream and not just include them, but to foreground their rich rawness and their diversity. Make them leaders, CEOs, head-hunters and recruiters, heads of state, policy makers and strategists; fill schools, hospitals, courts and committee rooms with them; break the unwritten codes; remake the fabric with raw, fragile threads. One of the most compelling cellists I ever heard had never been taught and was entirely, heart-stoppingly unformed.

And from this my eldest child, the setter of time, temperature and tide for the entire family, her younger sisters found their own relentless, restless energy, their staunchness, their fierce defence and consideration of and for others. And when self-belief takes a blow, lie low awhile and then come out of your corner, out from under your duvet. Those visits to hospitals up and down the land, our children sound in their beds, almost always ended with a whisky, or a few, to be precise. Maybe wrongly, they tell us. There are healthier, more dignified ways of overcoming fear, shock, disappointment; of dissipating anger; of hearing what you don't want to hear. Better ways of celebrating the successes too, or just drawing that line. However we choose to cope, to grow, to safeguard and carry us through and beyond that wall... with music, nicotine, a bumper pack of potato crisps or a spliff, it is the intimacy of unveiling, of stripping down; the articulated honesty, the absolute exposure that somehow in the quiet, brings solid resolve, slowly fills the void to the very top with a new strength. Brings back a glad eye, hilarity, wholeness; restores, brings a new self, and blessed, wondrous daylight.

It was important for me to seek permission from my daughter before writing this. I have never consistently confronted this history and never articulated any of this before. Working through the night, alone in an atelier in Provence earlier this year, I formed words and sentences to capture the feelings as they poured out.

Of all the words that I have ever produced these are by far the rawest. Whenever I stopped the flow or paused in any way, I found myself shaking, unable to speak. Whenever I reread it the tears still come. But both my writing and my daughter's reading of this piece, have exposed feelings in us both that neither of us ever fully explored, and brought about a conversation between us that we had never and certainly should have had. When it was done, I sent it to her. Anxious about her reaction, I couldn't wait for a response. It came within minutes: 'I realise, Mum, that we are both survivors,' she said. I had never thought of it that way. But we were and are.

There are occasions when there is nowhere to go, nowhere for us to hide; when what confronts you blocks your way, tall and menacing, like some dreadful mythological creature. But we have no option: 'I don't know how I will get through this, but I'll try'; we go forward. When there is nothing or no one on the outside to give you courage and strength, when your only option is to look deep into who you are, your own values, prejudices and the experiences that formed them, when the only way to acceptance is to deconstruct, to dismantle to connect with our feral instincts of survival first and foremost; to gather every particle of your being that is fit for the fight and in fear often and trepidation, you undertake the struggle and start to rebuild another self from the inside. My own journey towards some kind of acceptance is certainly not over. Nor is my daughter's. The writing of this piece has moved me on further. I am certainly not that superficial young woman that I was. Reconciliation and a reformulation of values is never easy.

Nothing, I believe, is ever greater than we are and we have choices in how we react. Yet, to overcome, to manage, to pull though, to regain solid, safe ground and some sort of new balance, to see a shaft of light, we become someone we didn't know or imagine. There is no doubt that trauma changes us, leaving us with a kind of branding. Whether for good or bad we live our lives with those marks burned into our very souls but at the same time too, we learn to live again. And maybe having gone through all of it, the suffering, anxiety, panic and terror, and the rage, our capacity to laugh, to weep and feel is the greater, our need to taste the fullness of existence and what life offers, the more compelling.

moonstruck

... and I know it is morning by the stillness rather than by the light. It settles me and ushers me into this new day. My movements are small and slight, such is my unwillingness to change even the tiniest detail of this perfect day, and as I lie low, on my back, gazing upwards, I welcome the rain. I am the rain that makes grass and leaves glisten. I am the hollow in thunder's boom. I am the cold moist earth grateful for a timid, probing sun. I am not a spectator and I feel somehow remade and whole once more – fragments, pieces of a jigsaw – returned to their rightful place, where everything fits together; by the mysteries of elusive trees or insistent, breaking waves; by bird flurries on a darkening, stormy sky; by cow dung, mud and glue and mating pigs, anointed. I want this to be my life now. The air that I breathe coaxes me comfortably and assuredly into the present moment and establishes my presence on this small patch of ground.

At a time of collapse and possibility, of choice and crossroads, I bought a tent. With no history or experience of camping and no discussion, I bought a tent. I had been heading in that direction for a few years, staking out hostels in Scotland and then further, to Norway and Iceland even. Up until that point my life had been more than comfortable and my career earned me privileges as did my salary. As a woman from an immigrant background, my birthright unfavourable, I had enjoyed the growing sense of achievement, winning, getting there, moving from post to post, on and on to where I felt I had reached the top. I went from classroom to national platform – I wanted to make a contribution to the many rather than the few – and from Citroën Dyane to BMW, from overdraft to platinum, from Edinburgh's Tollcross to Brussels and from teaching verb conjugations, guitar in hand, to Ministerial Task Force as 'expert'.

I enjoyed the frills: reserved parking spaces, the coffee in smart management suites, the swift disposing of my coat on arrival, the secretarial flurry. I was somebody. I had something to say. But then there became something quite distasteful about those years. Committed always to the cause and very much aware of the responsibility I carried, I enjoyed, indeed was fulfilled by the many high points of my work, but it did not take long for me to begin to feel uncomfortable about what I saw as power relationships – to observe the wielding of power both in attitude and bearing – and in the conduct of a number of processes, and sadly in relationships, professional and indeed personal, corrupted by wealth and/or status.

A very significant factor in this awakening, was also the part-time doctoral programme I had embarked on soon after joining Her Majesty's Inspectorate. It led me to question my own motives and behaviour. Those weeks when I became once again a student, attending seminars, riding a bicycle to the library, working on essays, a final thesis, in discussion with fellow professionals and most importantly, probing policy, statecraft and learning, sharpening my skills of critiquing, finding and feeling more at one with counter theory and rationales, all seemed in every way to provide a different perspective on my professional life. In some ways, it revealed the excessive consumerism of my own personal life as well.

As a scholar, liberated from political agendas, I was developing differently. I became more and more convinced of the importance of equality, the enormity and dignity of those we teach, what they can teach us, in the educational fabric and process; of dialogue and collaboration as a basis for every encounter, whether it be in governmental monitoring, policy making or classroom teaching. This dichotomy, this tension between two opposing lifestyles and two identities led me to some fundamental truths about myself.

So, I woke up one morning in Fort William having just completed The Great Glen Way, a 'walk across Scotland' from Inverness, of some 75 miles, and I needed air. I wanted another life. I had become weary and I had a sense of ending; another stage of my life completed; but that there was still much, much more. The notion of being a nomad, of being rootless and unharnessed, strongly appealed. And I bought a small tent without the faintest idea how to put it up or what to do next.

Anxiety is an affliction that I have struggled with for some years. It can range from fear of spiders crawling over my face while I sleep (I cannot lay aside information about the number of spiders we swallow in our sleep); to police at the door informing me of an accident involving one of my girls; to waking up paralysed, dumb or not waking up at all. I have yet to decide which is preferable: the growing knowledge that

*True guilt is guilt at the obligations one owes
to oneself to be oneself.* (RD Laing)

it's over for me, of losing that battle with each day, or
being fortuitously unaware of my final journey. I fear
my own unexpected tragedies. I fear the unwanted loss
of my known world.

Most of all I fear what, if anything, follows death.
Yet, strangely while camping alone, I never fear for
instance, the sudden appearance in the awning of
my tiny tent of a 'bad man' about to cut my throat,
or a crowd of drug-fuelled arseholes circling me
and forensically doing what they will, increasingly
aroused by my terror, *Clockwork Orange* style. Was
it Beethoven on the soundtrack? The horror of 'Ode
to Joy'? Exquisite music and gross brutality combined

The fact that I am postulating these scenarios I
guess, says that I have considered them, but for some
reason, while I am alone, albeit surrounded by other
kindly campers, in a field or on a beach, these thoughts
never arise. I have slept with roaring East Coast seas
virtually lapping at my ground sheet threshold, tsunami
style; been sandwiched between large mobile homes
that in storms might have fallen over and crushed my
little green makeshift and me within it; slumbered
deep with lightning directly above my head, metal
poles holding my sturdy wee construction together,
with gales that have bent my air beams and did once
bring my voluminous large tent down necessitating

a crawling crab action to retrieve our valuables; and the wildernesses of mist on moorland and the absence of light or any sign of a living soul, so bad was the visibility.

The reason for my insouciance in dire, at times even dangerous circumstances that might scare the most hardy, I think, is that the very act of putting myself in a highly volatile and changeable situation where the outcome, my fate is unknown or threatened: a sudden gale or thunderstorm, the unavailability of somewhere to buy food, the failure of a tent pole or a sudden gash in the tent, acts as a kind of rebalancing. It sets the emotive meter back to zero, where the contortions of the imaginative and fearful brain become so remote, so outrageous, that they fade into the unreality, into the largely implausible arena that they come from; and the very immediate possibilities and practicalities of life and survival come back into view, are re-established and become the central focus.

Hilary Mantel's Reith Lectures were far from my mind on the morning that I sat in a queue to board the ferry from Uig in Skye, to Tarbert on the Isle of Harris. My tent was neatly packed away in the car boot, along with all the other basics for survival, soft sleeping, one-click cooking, various foldaways, couscous... courtesy of a seasoned traveller I met once who advised it for any salad anytime, anywhere for eateries in Scotland are often erratic... sometimes yes and sometimes no... it's past lunch hour... the cook's gone home... we're out of season... yes open, no we are not... a dish of peanuts maybe...? A corkscrew too and the possibility of a dram or two.

I had gloriously carefree and unplanned days ahead

A word is a bridge thrown between myself and another. (Ivana Marková)

of me to meander through the Hebrides alone with my thoughts, books, notebooks and a precious ferry timetable (no bookings, no pressure), single- handedly setting up and settling where I landed, with only the rain or sun to move me on, the sight of bright, sprite machair, all the yellows of morning light; beaches of indigo and red in the aftersun; the floating landscapes of water lilies on still, shady pools; or perhaps an old, crumbling wall, the tragic story of a cleared house or an old church, its flagstones worn with the tread of centuries, to pull me in, a moonlit ruin to keep me. So, with nothing better to do, the kind-eyed, weathered ferryman in his box, as yet not in action, I was slowly drawn into 'The Day is For the Living' (BBC, June 2017).

The notion of the dead being accessible, in some way or other, that they are with us always, are voiced, given form, mediated and interpreted by us, has remained with me since that afternoon listening to Mantel's very precise, fruity delivery, surrounded as I was by camper vans, jeeps tied with rope, Harley Davidson bikes, transport lorries, dogs and discarded paper cups. I think it such a warming idea and it makes sense, for at the very worst times of my life, I feel my mother; her presence; her breath on me; not that I somehow long for her comforting bosom (she didn't do comfort easily) but I hear her voice, throaty, clear and directive.

At any major life event, I am convinced that our ancestors are indeed at the door. We embody them as a part of who we are or become. Mantel puts it well. Buddhist thinking is clear. Whether it is the abandoning of all and everyone I know, the slow pace of life in remote places, the focus on what is important – burying the dead (a formal dignified showing); buying the fish from the harbour for dinner, baking your bread, rounding up the sheep – that sudden departure from my usual, my life lived in cities, clears and stills my mind, encourages me to pause and focus, to imagine and construct, to see my life in new, unexpected and potential contexts, to visualise what might be. That *décalage* or gear drop, creates a void, an empty expanse, prime for the filling, an impulse to embrace, experiment, a new lifescript, ways to go and ways to be.

And the prompts are all around in those that I talk to and observe, just living their lives: the artists and groupies on Skye or North Uist, their pure, flowing wool and heather-toned tweeds; the ruddy barman at Lochboisdale chatting to the habitual, gloomy gathering of whisky boys at 3.00pm, or indeed the lone drinker; the cheery, back-slapping young men in from the boats in Tarbert or in the Fisherman's Mission in Mallaig, their boots still wet, eating their fish and chips; keen-eyed, hardy and wise, local women, fresh-faced still at 50, selling crumbly home-baked scones bulging with fruit or grainy, rich lentil soup in some coffee spot on Barra or the heritage centre in Lismore; a young artisan in the back of their grocer's shop selling undyed wool from her own sheep; men serving food on the CalMac ferries and their old-school politeness; the Doc Marten-shod, abundantly tattooed 20-somethings with pink or blue hair, fresh home from Glasgow University. Each has a story, each has a lifestyle, each can show, teach me something new.

While it gives me huge pleasure to camp with those close to me, partner, family and friends and these have been wonderfully relaxed and intimate holidays, camping alone however, with no distractions of conversation no enormity of another presence or discourse, no other commentary or agenda to confuse my thinking or block my fanciful imagining, the contact and impact of strangers and surroundings is more forceful and direct. Alone, I am more receptive, open, and more susceptible; I hear and see more clearly. I am neutral, uncoloured, washed clean of my history. I can identify, imitate, become.

It was on Westray, one of the Orkney Isles, that I first learned about Ursula le Guin, the feminist sci-fi writer from a young man, an archaeologist who was working on a project there. How wonderful to be a young archaeologist digging for the past, analysing findings in order to summon old civilisations. Is this a degree I could now consider? And in the face of that, the vision of me, in ripped, canvas trousers, sweating profusely as trowel in hand, in Heraklion, I bring up three gold coins, floats through my mind. What a boring life is this! My predictable career, as nothing; meaningful yes, but desperately ordinary. Confronted with that, I said little. Though to my credit, while on a college inspection in Kirkwall, Orkney, unlike my worthy colleagues, poring over notes, I burst through the swing doors at lunchtime, out, out, out into the open and took my sandwiches every day to St Magnus Cathedral where I sat alone and munching, surrounded by wonderful red and yellow sandstone of 850 years history and a lovely organ, almost 100 years old.

And it was a precise kind of woman, neurotically counting and recounting tins, packs of meat and bread rolls in preparation for a walk into the Knoydart peninsula with, I guessed, a new-found manfriend, that caught my attention and that led me there myself some years after, and many times since. The joy and excitement of a fellow camper in Mallaig determined my quite recent, long distance cycle trip from Barra to Skye in the Outer Hebrides, later to cycling in the Orkney islands; and it was a chance encounter with a generous, grieving woman who offered her bike in South Uist that led me to writing seriously, changed the direction of my life and both of us to poetry friendship. While washing my breakfast dishes in the communal facilities hut at Horgabost campground on the Isle of Harris, I even got the heads-up for where to find good coffee in Perth, not easy there or indeed anywhere north of the central belt; and where to find the best smoked salmon on Lewis.

These more or much less profound encounters, many of them, too numerous to note, these chance conversations in community centres, bookshops, town halls at local sales of work where I have seen the art of soap making, shearing sheep, needlecraft, and hand spun wool; ceilidhs, where the men are offered whisky and the ladies a sherry, all have gradually over time, eroded a lifestyle and contributed to who I am for now.

I live in a city, I inhabit other selves elsewhere; on the one hand, a carefully balanced meal planned ahead, maybe an Ottolenghi jewel, an Anna Jones appetiser or a cucumber infused cocktail from *The Guardian* weekend pages; on the other, a what-the-hell, packet of corned beef, tortilla chips and tinned peas bought at a general food outlet behind a garage in Invergarry; the same contradictions in dress and form. It would be as laughable for me to eat dinner in a Tom Kitchin bistro in my all-weather, multi-pocket roughwear and Teva sandals, complete with fedora style rain hat, as it would to wear a sleek, Swedish black number on the Culbin Sands and the rough wash of the Western tides.

While morning on Uig Bay on the Isle of Lewis, offers redemption, opportunity for recovery of what has been lost, for repair; is charged with a new bond with all terms and conditions altered. A smoky late afternoon, as we totter back, of corks popping, laughter and gatherings; of homing and familiar; of wood and barbecue; of tossed down walking shoes and mountain bikes, of airing feet, the to and fro from fresh water taps; of buckets and ball games; the fetching of ice, the expanse of lush, green ground by Loch Morlich, near Aviemore, a different and contented stillness hanging in the air, brings a sense of release, of letting go and of resignation. There is no more to prove today, nothing more to manage. We reconcile with what has passed and slip easily into endings.

...'Look, look up,' she said and I saw the moon. And our small world, each of us living our respective adventures within it, breathes one long contented sigh. Harmony settles and we drift hazily into night time together. Voices quieten and unruly dogs flop, and the only sound is the occasional crackle of logs, someone snoring. In this place, for now at least, where people are generous, where grass feathers black, the red moon is plump with bounty. Tonight we are replete with a craft beer, a choc ice and a sausage or two. Every tomorrow brings opportunity and especially when we are quiet.

Life is ever rich and exciting. There are always new worlds and new ways of being. All we need to do is to look up.

game-changer

... food welcomes the new day. A fragrant *pastina in brodo* (small pasta shapes in broth) with just a few fresh herbs and an olive oil softened onion, will rouse you from your flu and make your achiness, whether it be menstrual, viral or exercise overload, a bit better. It will soothe a hangover or hurt pride. It will restore balance and equilibrium. Yoga in a bowl, no less. If you feel adventurous, you might drop a beaten egg into the soothing broth. The stuff of magma and volcanoes, of seismic movement of the earth, sea and plummeting of the stars, this basic broth harks back to the ancestors, when life was altogether different. When there was no packaging, no commodifying, no dictats on the percentaging of nutrients. When food was not fodder for headline grabbing politicians on the up. When food was not an industry but the means of surviving by cultivating and gathering what was available and the knowing wisdom and skills of good women.

Modern technology makes a science of food. Contemporary chefs make artistic mosaics on a plate. For me, fine dining is a rather bland, over-sanitised experience, often stripped of its cultural origins. It is clearly not for me. Nothing, I believe, can better a lively palate, instinctive risk taking in both producing food and tasting it, dishes that are unsurpassable through their innocence, wholesomeness and the energy and passion of the cook. That is true delight.

Food is a world in itself, a universe of magnificent diversity ranging across a wide spectrum of ingredients, taste, customs and culture, terms of reference and even language. Its magical appeal and strength lie both in difference and at the same time, similarity. How to cook eggs or chicken for example.

My Italian grandmother used to gently poach eggs in a sauce of fresh tomatoes which she reheated from our standard Sunday spaghetti. Turkish menemen and Middle Eastern shakshuka are altogether more peppery versions of that childhood dish and I suspect theirs was the original version, with the wonderful base additions of onions and peppers, chilli, cumin and ground coriander.

A roasted chicken will have many, many presentations throughout the world, many stuffings too. Though my preference is what I saw done many times at home: a sauté of onions, walnuts and dried fruit added, then breadcrumbs and marjoram, all bound together by Parmesan and a beaten egg.

My all-time favourite chicken dish is Palestinian musakhan chicken which I cooked for a family meal one Christmas. The chicken is jointed and marinaded in wonderful Eastern spices, including lemon juice and sumac and then laid on a bed of onions and placed in the oven. When the chicken is almost cooked through, large sheets of flatbreads are warmed and laid on a platter with the cooked chicken, caramelised onions and all the pan juices placed on top. The combination of spice infused soft dough, dripping with juice and the yielding flesh of the meat tucked within its folds is an experience that will always remain with me. The elemental eating of it with everyone grasping and clutching handfuls off the platter was a spectacle to watch and deeply, gutfully satisfying.

It was my prolonged stay in Italy in my 20s that marked my first real encounter with the compulsive and forceful appeal of food; its sensuality and importance in our lives. Its emotional and cultural significance, its power were very clear throughout my childhood. Lying on a wall in searing Mediterranean sunshine outside a small stone house, its walls crumbling, only a table and chairs, a single bed and a cooker inside, a dog barking and hens off astray in a dusty, cluttered yard, an overwhelming, mouth-watering smell made me perk up. I was accustomed to lusty cooking smells of course, but this was altogether grander, not to be taken lightly or ignored. What followed was a wonderful *pappardelle al sugo di pomodori* with fat hunks of soft bread and a cracking crust for mopping up.

On another occasion, that same loaf, gone stale, steeped in virgin olive oil from the nearby olive trees, leavened by fresh tomato chunks warmed in sunshine, wine vinegar, salt, onions, sliced garlic and olives from the same trees... *panzanella,* Molise style. Is there anything more glorious than rustic bread laden with vinegar or lemon juice, olive oil and the sweet ooze and seeds of Mediterranean tomatoes? Nothing in the world tastes like those ordinary, everyday tomatoes, the more misshapen, the better, hardy and hearty, like its fine people. Fresh figs from the communal orchard completed that lovely meal.

Many recipes, versions of rustic, in restaurants and

the pages of weekend magazines for foodies aim to reproduce, enhance, indeed compete, with such humble fair. For me, the naked, unsullied original wins every time. A few years later, living in the Aveyron area of France, well-respected for its culinary elegance and grace, I was again taken unawares: by the prime importance of newly baked bread, *pain de campagne*, for my *tartines*, wonderful homemade jam less sugared than our own home brands, the spongy receptivity of both, when paired, and dunked in the sweetness and warming depths of a milky coffee.

I found myself titillated by the subtle texture of *pommes mousseline* (not to be compared with ordinary old mash but suggestively translucent, moist and smooth), when well executed, an elegant first layer on which to lay down whatever else might accompany it; and designed to offer a soft counterpoint, a creamy coating for whatever it partners. I discovered provençal honey and thyme then too. Among the lavender expanses of the southern French countryside, I learned about the difference between a *pintade*, guinea fowl, and a chicken. *Pintade* is finer boned and its meat softer if slow-cooked *languedoc* style. It is altogether, lighter, more delicate than its clumsy relative.

My education in cheese too started in France and in particular in the specifics of a good Roquefort, the king of all cheeses, though only sovereign and at its best when eaten in its home area. I have never tasted as good since. The secret of its rich perfection is of course, apart from the distribution and density of blue veining, the delicate balance between hard and crumbly... not too much of one or the other. It should be almost spreadable, never firm, it should topple, rather than be sliced.

My relationship and journey with food, as for many, has posed some challenges too. The link between food and psychological, emotional health is now well recognised and help is available, but was not at when I was in my late teens. Food then, became a means of disappearing. The less appealing I felt I was, the less appealing I made myself, so that I would be even less visible. In that way, my self-loathing, would not even be noticed. As the 'plain, morosely brainy child', as a young adult I chose to be relegated. This sad situation was not helped by a family of women who flaunted their sexuality and looks and in particular, a mother whose objective it was to be noticed and to be gauged and weighed up for her powers of attraction. I might have coped with that, though it did 'shrink' me even more, but what I found more wounding was that when people gushed and complimented her, her figure, her glamour, they cast a regretful eye in my direction and said not a word. My mother in full sail, did not seem to notice. She loved the acclamations, did not even stop to consider the impact on me.

While my contemporaries talk nostalgically about their teenage years, their first kiss, first flurries in the backseat of a car, I see things a little differently. I do not want to remember those years. I did not so much binge, as take refuge in food without any regard for how much I actually needed, or was good for me. It was a first love encounter that settled me down, gave me some of the confidence I needed, to feel attractive and wanted and that my body, which had always caused me chagrin and discomfort, could give and experience pleasure. I lost weight and found my fascination with clothes and joy in fitting them; the thrill of exploring fashion, and some outré extravaganzas of presentation.

An eating problem surfaced again in my early to mid-20s. This time, I went on what I can only describe as a kind of hunger strike, starving myself to the point of debility and dizziness and then eating as much chocolate and biscuits as I could pack in. I had to take time off work. The doctor's advice was to ensure that I was eating nourishing food but I was losing weight quite quickly, which pleased me. My favourite thing was to feel my hip bones every night as I settled into sleep. Those days have long passed. I have to say that finding my hip bones now, might be more of a risky expedition, requiring a fair quantity of patience and technical support for the task.

Through the years, food has been a strong indicator of my state of mind. Like my low level, continual anxiety, what I eat or don't eat has been a nagging issue. I wrestle with the tensions between maintaining a weight which allows me to wear what I love best and at the same time, enjoying the immense pleasure of lovely dishes with friends and family, of finding a pleasing place to eat out in, of cooking whatever I fancy, or creating feasts for those I love.

All of this inner conflict has lessened over time. Maturity brings many unforeseen benefits. Maybe through motherhood, looking beyond my own needs, maybe through the distractions of career and life events generally I have found some core stability, and cope better with how I am seen or not seen by others. I have developed a gentle acceptance of the limitations of my own body and its appearance and an acknowledgement of my vulnerabilities. Some failed friendships have made me reflect on my faults but in a constructive way.

An awareness of my fears can still overwhelm me, but with help, with affirming messages of belief in me and in my abilities, I can retrieve some self-confidence. I am not in shadow any longer. Maybe I present too brightly for some. To put things simply, I no longer reach for a chocolate bar if someone fails to say hello or I don't get a response to my email. Instead, I might seek to find out why. Food then, for me at least, is an entirely intimate matter, a fulfilling relationship – my attitude and approach to it a barometer – a measure of my mental health; of happiness and security; of how I see my place, my contribution and worth; my degree of comfort within society and within my friendship and family circles.

On Holy Isle, the Buddhist centre near the Scottish Isle of Arran, the warm exchanges of humour and life experiences following a vegan minestrone of my own making for 20 or so guests, have led to lifetime, loving friendships, to new reading, to finding a new course and seeing a fresh horizon. And as I set down my reheated linguine, done in a touch of hot virgin oil in a shallow pan to the point of crustiness, an extravagant mound of rigatoni (our symbols of family reunion) lightly rinsed through with my own simple bolognese, the generous pasta tubes gorged with meaty flavour, topped with a lick of mascarpone and dotted with small explosions of cherry tomatoes and fresh oregano or basil, the thundering unspoken response tells me that I love and am loved by my family in return. That I have come this far.

Food plays a key role in easing connections, creating communion; cooked with dedication, care and heart, it is a means of opening yourself up and bringing, letting others in. Good food, plenty of it, accompanied by outrageous laughter, with friends, is surely unparalleled as a way of making everyone feel good, of belonging, of feeling part of something and of putting any negative thoughts or experiences behind you, of fading them out.

There is so much healing in a plate or a pot. Setting down a worthy antipasto cannot fail... made up of maybe, marinaded mushrooms and walnuts which have been soaking all day in a heady cocktail of balsamic vinegar or lemon juice and virgin olive oil with garlic, with perhaps a platter of pale pink pistachio-studded, tenderest mortadella, paper-thin, stretched slices of Serrano ham or San Daniele, which you could swallow in a gulp, and which require no chewing or knife, stuffed mushrooms or red peppers, baked to crinkled, cracked perfection, topped with a crisp crust of golden Parmesan and breadcrumbs. These delights enjoyed with friends, will bring out the best version of you and create the very best of vibes in a room, and in its very walls, for good times leave their mark. Good food makes histories. Washed down with a glass of dark-hearted Argentinian Malbec or a chunky Pugliese Primitivo, a Nero D'Avola even, they will loosen your tongue, give you ears and perspective. There can be no better way of coming together, of creating the conditions for honest talk, of discovering another soul. Of deepening and looking into your own.

To take pleasure in and fully appreciate the food of any country, besides simply wanting to be fed, it is important to have a sense of adventure. It is important to be open, to value the traditions that created it, and the social practices that surround it. Cold-blooded cooks with little passion and unyielding horizons will never truly satisfy lusty stomachs and nor will companions who seem to forget that eating is the reason for sitting at a table. Food changes behaviour too. In restaurants throughout these British Isles, we might see spaghettini eaten with only a spinning fork, chopsticks so skilfully twirled in France or elsewhere that even the smallest grain of rice poses little problem; and in Glasgow perhaps or some other Scottish city, kitchens woks are commonplace. Or, they certainly are, in the West (or best) End. The current demand for small plates, bites and tapas style food has led us, demanding seekers of good, cheap eats, to abandon the formulaic, lock-step French tradition of individual courses and to eat whatever comes when, so that our table is never bare and there are always enticing choices before us to seduce. Best of all for some (me included), rather like toddlers splashing gleefully through puddles, increasingly eat with their hands, joyfully mopping, munching, and dipping.

Crunchy fattoushes, grainy, moist tabbouleh full of herby zest and colour, bubbling, hearty tagines, unctuously soothing labneh, invite us not just to cook or eat, but to, for an hour or so, respectfully enter into at least the spirit of abundant heritage and to leave behind our own. Food speaks a culture, a history and a civilisation. Imprinted on the food of Palestine, Lebanon and Eastern climes, are still, beyond war and holocaust, the proud traces of the hands of scarved women who milled the flour, kneaded the bread, stirred the pots, gutted the wildfowl, nurtured the spices and worked the soil. The food on your table is the result of what has been handed down through generations, through ritual, through famine and droughts, the distilled essence of festivals and religious ritual. It is the product of a precious ancient universe, whose precepts, philosophies and traditions laid down the societal structures, from which the Western world grew. These old ways created the dazzling array of dishes that adorns your table as you sit, maybe on cushions around a circular table, sipping mint tea.

When I make spring rolls or gulp my pho straight from the bowl, I bow to other ways of thinking, to other ways of conceiving existence. I bow to freshness, to delicacy and the lightest of touches ensuring that the food I am consuming or preparing is largely undisturbed and remains intact.

Food has a persuasive voice suggesting that we think and behave differently. We can choose not to, of course, like those ex-pats near Malaga on a Christmas Day, sitting on a beach, wearing paper hats and eating turkey; or the seekers of TV soaps and sun who visit the Algarve in white sun gear, sports shorts and outlandish sunglasses, looking for a fry-up. Food challenges your ways, your taste buds and often your constitution. It invites change. And it may only be a short step from grilled fish in Porto or a fragile filo-crusted leek pie in Ithaca to a new interest, and a new language.

Food can of course be a highly sensitive and political issue, a social marker. In towns and cities all over the world there are eateries of different ethnicities, established by people from other lands who have made that country their home. Theirs however, can be a volatile, somewhat precarious position depending on political overturns and global waves of ideological change and the impact on how they and their birth country are regarded by the local dominant culture or the small town politics of the local business community. Sometimes these cafés and restaurants pop up in response to the needs of their own ethnic communities. Better still, good fortune may pave the way for them to infiltrate the establishment, even alter local preferences and food choices, transform and radically alter old habits. Such was the experience of the Italian communities who have settled in the UK since the 19th century. Established and content in their local communities, well-loved for all their differences and to all intents and purposes integrated, as a result of the political outturn in the late '30s and '40s during WW2, their fortunes metamorphosed overnight: individuals and communities were ostracised, families became the new 'enemy', weasels in the hen coop, struggled to survive.

It took many years for them to re-establish their position. But the influence of Italians and the food culture they brought, their impact on the hospitality industry worldwide, has been enormous. Consider now, the international appreciation of pizza, pasta, ice cream; of Aperol and prosecco; and how many of us drink a rich, distinguished espresso to kick the day into action. And though preparation remains a mystery for most, polenta and gnocchi both sit proudly on supermarket shelves. Polenta still seen as an Oliver replacement for oven chips, becomes an oozing, velvety porridge and when topped with a rich tomato sauce that has been slowly developing on the lowest flame of your gas hob, large shavings of pecorino, seasoned with garlic, maybe a little sautéed onion and a fresh green herb, it settles the mind and feeds your very core.

But where, in a small French town or in New York

for example, Indian, Chinese, Lebanese, non-European or non-indigenous foods are to be found, also tells its own story. The presence and ready availability of these fabulous foods, colours, adds character and loud bustle to the streets of our cities and brightens your morning. The aromas from the kitchens will tempt you to a curry no matter the time of day. A food list in the window of a Vietnamese restaurant makes the heart sing. It is a matter of celebration when they are not located within the limited confines of a subculture; in an untended and unfrequented street, separated off; part of a string of restaurants, cheek by jowl not only competing against prevailing taste, but worse still, against each other. In an ideal setting there are no Chinatowns, but rather, a well-doing, respected ethnic cuisine, sitting alongside the city's best, offering another cuisine and way of eating to an integrated, open-minded, welcoming and above all, civilised society.

There are many ways to get under the skin of a country as many have found and many ways in which a country can get under yours and sweep you off your feet and change you forever. In a Sicilian village for instance, it might be attending Sunday Mass, observing the practice, the demographic of the congregation, listening to the mighty 18th century organ, the readiness of people to sing the hymns; and whether at key points of liturgy, people kneel or stand. These observations tell us something about the people and the social mores surely. The interior of a light-filled, lofty, Lutheran church in Norway nudges us into maybe a reflection on the positivity, delicacy and hope of such a religion and the mindset of its followers. In Cuba or in Costa Rica staying with a family, living the everyday, might cause us to question our own way of life. And in Scotland, maybe, a visit to Skye and hearing a pibroch, might call up a fresh desire for deep personal change: a change of lifestyle, approach, perceptions, political viewpoint or values. Those insights and the impact of them may be the triggers for radical re-positioning and profound internal re-ordering.

Food, as an everyday occurrence tells its own story. Watching two young French women recently at a bistro in Provence, I realised how much upbringing forms our own attitudes to food; I understood France better. I admired it, its customs, values and way of life even more. Well-founded in family traditions of fresh, good food, there was no dizzy page turning of menus, no hesitancy, no hyperventilating and no sense of wonder, only quiet anticipation of a good meal; and very pragmatically, they chose a precise *haché* and an orangutang-sized burger. Without even a glance at the drinks list, they named their separate wines of choice and when the food arrived, without comment, got on with the serious business of eating, drinking and chatting. This was a canon and a protocol they knew well, had been reared with.

In watching people eat, we learn so much, we see better ways and we grow. Food is a lens through which we see more clearly, to the heart of things. We make comparisons, we see other points of view and we make changes. We do not stand still.

In the current climate, a great deal of rhetoric and debate surrounds the issue of immigration. As someone from an immigrant family who has contributed her best effort to the country my grandparents chose to live in, I stand wholly and uncompromisingly committed to multiculturalism and a plural society. A society of mixed but not ghettoised ethnicity. Not simply through a sense of loyalty to my own background but because there is strong evidence to show the benefits of plurality, of a coherent society of rich diversity and of shared identities. In that diverse world, there surely is less of 'them' and 'us'. More fundamentally still, experts claim that those who think beyond national boundaries, those who embrace a holistic, complex view of different cultures and their languages, those who are open to exploring cultural diversity, hybridity and interconnections, stand more ready and able to discover and liberate their own creative repertoire. They have an altogether different, wider view and vision. They are known to possess increased cognitive flexibility and they see into issues from more of a questioning rather than a fixed, implacable position.

To move beyond cultural difference, to move into and absorb other cultures is an exciting way of performing and expressing our humanity, being open to influence and transacting positively across divides. I believe that food and all that surrounds it, its protocols and customs, the agriculture and industries that accompany it, has the potential to provide that gateway.

Eating represents more than mere consumption, it can become instead, a means of effective transaction across race; a gentle and pleasing open highway of personal evolution. It is multi-faceted: both a game-changer and catalyst, a champion and symbol, a relic of time past, a reliquary for memory and tradition, a marker and signifier of social position and background and a powerful force for individual as well as societal change and discovery. For it is through months spent in France and Italy (where different varieties of onions, lettuce and tomatoes each have a purpose, where cheese is bought either for tonight or for a month hence and avocados either for today or tomorrow), eating the dishes of wonderful, warm-hearted home cooks, my own journeying from the Readers Digest cookbook for beginners through to Marcella Hazan's lamb dishes and *caponata*, and the splendid array of cookbooks from the Levant and other continents, that I succumbed to an enlightenment, a revelation, and the properties of a heavy bottomed marmite or pan and all it can do.

The matter of food is of such moment, that a last meal is a recognised concession for a condemned prisoner; encouraged in hospices where the end is not far off; a marker of rites of passage and past, and current rituals of every society and generation.

Food is a crowning, a blessing on a wonderful experience or day, a token of love and commitment, a preamble to lovemaking, a sealing of shared moments. The breaking of bread, drinking from the same cup is both an agape and a token of reconciliation. Its ability to give pleasure, to heal; to create enjoyment, laughter and friendship, provide the highlights of a weekend or a holiday; its ability to make you smile, bring you back to concrete reality and a hold on life again at the saddest of times. Most significantly, for the purpose of a full and rich existence always ahead and available, of a society that looks outwards and transcends frontiers, food is a *lingua franca*, a personal adventure of fluidity, growth, and continual opportunity. And always only an hour or two away.

On a personal note, in another life I might well have been be a chef. If there is another life to come, I will be. For I cannot resist the appeal of a kitchen.

It is a setting where I feel at home and at ease. Finding my usual space in my kitchen with all I need around me and spending a low-key afternoon, out of the swim and cooking dish after dish from time to time, is healing. When the birth of my granddaughter was imminent, for no apparent reason, though I had no plan whatsoever to eat pasta, feeling a kind of stirring in my innards, I took to the kitchen. I love the creative space of a kitchen, its contrasts... starkness, science and hardware and the wonderful smells that fill it and cling to the very walls of the house, saying 'come in; you are so welcome'; or 'I love you'; 'look at what I have prepared for us to enjoy together'. For there is no doubting that an aroma enveloping you as you stand to be greeted in a doorway, or waiting for a door to open, fills you with such well-being that unconsciously makes you smile; a welcoming waft of something good to eat draws you in, in a way that no words can.

My kitchen is a palette where I can work at texture, blend colours, and where I consider very carefully, ever tasting, maybe with a wee glass or two, what combinations of taste, arresting, surprising and sensual, will reach down into the very soul and arouse a gluttonous frenzy. The theatre and drama of it, the opportunity for the unexpected all excite me. Kitchens are such positive places where stories are made, poetry is written, murals, triptychs, organ symphonies and chorales that raise the roof emanate from stove to table.

I cook when I need balance, when I need to be grounded, when I am at peace with the world, when I am too overcome to speak, when I cannot contain the love; and its flows copiously into a sauté pan; when some grandstanding is demanded, or quite simply when preparations for the arrival of someone I enjoy, are expedient.

To cook as part of a team is a different experience: a deadline, a common goal brings with it, that welcome feeling of being a part of something, of intimacy and sharing; it offers a perspective on the big and small matters in your life, and through that dependency one on the other, highlights your strengths when you come to someone's rescue, time not on your side and also your weaknesses when you can't really be bothered to mop that floor and turn your attention instead to drying dishes. Too much turmeric or chilli in your stew, a sauce that will not thicken... and someone averts that disaster for you and you feel a rush of gratitude, even tears; that is an historic shared moment never to be forgotten. *MasterChef* aside, yes indeed, let me be a cook! Come forth all you millionaires, let me open restaurants and this will be my afterlife!

What is the best pizza you might ask? My answer is ever the same: a basic, well fired dough, in a home oven, sprinkled with no more than fresh tomatoes, olive oil and garlic. This for me is where my *affaire* started.

fika

...I do not like parties. Or should I say that I do not enjoy gatherings where people who don't know each other stand around making conversation. In fact, I don't like coffee breaks much either... just happy to get on with the job in hand. In my Edinburgh Colinton years, we had dinner parties very regularly, mainly for business and professional associates. It was a *thing* then. I loved the whole lead-up and preparation, the theatre of it: the planning of dishes and treats, the shopping for delicacies, the look of the cheese board oozing and glistening, candlelight on a well-turned out dinner table, the final verdict on what I might wear and the hard sweat in the kitchen as I assembled, on one occasion 23 salads.

All done, scene set, I would retire to my room and get myself ready, usually with a little something to put me in the mood... maybe a gin and tonic or a *negrone*, a vicious blend of alcohols and hugely effective if you want to get a party started. Then the doorbell would ring and still not completely dismissing the idea of climbing out of the window and running away, I would slowly cross the room with an air of composure that masked the nervy growl in my tummy.

The issue for me is I am uncomfortable or find it difficult to open up conversation with people I don't know and I find the words used to do that hardly worth saying. These are not occasions where, for me, real conversation takes place and so, while I know that most of the rest of the world happily engages in these social rituals, I question their value. Given just a little more time, two easy chairs and a quiet corner, so much more could be gained.

I was once invited to attend a 'networking' event for new writers at the Edinburgh Book Festival.

As I entered the Events Tent, I saw two people I knew engaged in conversation. Great I thought. Wine in hand, I went over full of good cheer. They just continued to talk to each other while I listened. It was as if I wasn't there. After tolerating this behaviour for a few minutes, telling myself that they were just socially inept with no idea how to conduct themselves at such events, I walked away, and this time, joined a group where I knew no one. Great interest in who I was etc. But then, after the minute I was granted to introduce myself, they resumed their previous conversation and once again, I found myself excluded, consigned to the background unable to get a word in and without a clue as to what they were talking about. I grabbed one more drink, drank it in one, sweetly said goodnight, walked around the corner to a Chinese restaurant and took myself out to dinner where I met two lovely men with whom I chatted all night.

Not long ago, I went to a Buddhist retreat centre near Bordeaux for a week. On the final day, we all gathered for a celebratory lunch, vegan and delicious. Meals were always taken in silence and so we collected our food from the kitchen and sat outside in a beautifully sunny garden. Naturally, we migrated towards those we had spent time with through the week. There were two women, one from Monaco who sold antiques and another a teacher of English from the North of France both of whose company I had really enjoyed. In fact, the antique dealer and I had shared what I can only describe as a 'cave', the walls rough and cold in November.

Sprightly she was and after each sitting session, I would return to where we slept to find her stretched out on the ground easing her back. She had come to the centre in order to start thinking about how she might prepare for death though she was not dying. Far from it. But I won't forget that last lunch. We sat together, all three, in total silence, utterly bonded, in complete communication for the best part of an hour; it was of course a parting and the emotional flow between us was palpable. At the end, we stood, hugged and tearful the teacher said just two words '*bonne route*', may you travel your road well. The phrase was short and simple yet it said all that was needed. We had exchanged contact details but never got in touch. Words would have been too little and too trivial for what we had given, learned and shared.

Behind me just now is a group of French women learning conversational English. We are in a coffee shop in a southern French town where I am spending a few weeks. While coffee drinking is extensive across continental Europe, and in particular maybe in France, coffee shops as we in the UK understand them, places for a good toasty brew... soft and foamy, thick and murky... for chat-ups, meet-ups and a slew of laptops are not common in France.

You can't *flâner* or mooch about in a café in France.

*Never resist a sentence you like, in which
language it takes its own pleasure and in
which, having abused it for so long, you are
stupefied by its innocence.* (Jean Baudrillard)

Waiters get nervous and at lunchtime especially, at
that sacramental hour of gourmandise and grace, you
will most definitely not be welcome, no matter how
good you look. Though the manner of removing you
might differ a little. You can do certain things in cafés:
read a serious newspaper such as *Le Monde*, smoke
a small cigar, well-scarved and iconic you can stare at
the goings on in the street, thumb an elegant book, all
these things are allowed; but you cannot just 'hang'.
And this little place, where I currently am, an *anticafé*,
all Ercol furniture and cool colour, in rue Granet, in
the heart of the old town of Aix-en-Provence, a warm
corner of welcome and easy chic, is an exception.
Furthermore, as a French café which also acts as a
little centre of cultural activities, language exchange,
reading and discussion groups: well, this is a new one
on me too, though I could be wrong. I have come to
Aix principally to write undisturbed; no worries about
servicing the boiler or cleaning the windows.

My other reason for coming to France generally is
because I want to recapture something I once had and
that over the years, has been eroded; a lost identity
one might say, or one that got buried among all the
competing others. So, I have come alone, and have been
completely alone for some days. And when visitors
arrive in the next weeks, the deal is that my alone time

will remain the priority and all else will be planned around it.

As a result of these days and nights on my own, with no sustained conversation, only the mundane transactions of buying food, paying for coffee or a white port, getting a bus ticket, saying hello to the neighbours, I woke up the other day to find my head full of not English, but unrelated and somewhat random French words.

It took a while for me to realise that these were indeed French words; suddenly I thought 'I'm thinking in French' and it was almost as if there had been so much packed in there during the previous days, and evidently so little space for any more, the words poured out, an eruption, slowly at first and then in a starburst... and like a mad thing, I began to speak the words in my head out loud, like an actor rehearsing lines, saying them over and over as I wandered around my little *atelier*, my work space. As I did that, then other words followed and they tumbled out in rapid flow as if I had popped a cork... words I had heard during this new time in France, new phrasings or new ways of saying things; and unprompted words that came from nowhere: the French for light switch, bathroom pipe, laundry, clothes hanger, light bulb and then all the adverbs with which people seemed to start their sentences: *assurément, évidemment, justement, précisément*; and words I had known and forgotten and bizarrely, didn't need right at that very moment. They just presented themselves, one by one, as if to say, we are here if you need us and there's more there if you want.

I have of course visited France many times since my

first time, a defining time, all those years ago but never alone and it has always been for a holiday. And during that first time, that year, with no English speaking buddies, through observing people and listening to conversation, through a thorough consideration of what it is to be French, I did all I could to become French myself... in my presentation, manner and speech. It is with some pride that I remember the disdain with which I was spoken to in Paris because of my fruity, *languedoc* accent and cadence.

There is a distinct difference between speaking a language, putting words together and being fluent; and again, between fluency and inhabiting a language, making it authentic and making it your own. To truly live within and absorb a language, new words, pronunciations and idioms, and to invite a language to take root within you, as is the case with our own mother tongue, we always confront new words and phrases. It is linguistic authenticity and ownership that matter.

Language skills aside, what is needed for the fluidity and versatility that characterise mastery of a language, is a total, willing shift of intellectual, cultural and personal position; a welcoming in of otherness and a will to blend and broaden the scope of who we are. We evolve in language. If we are too buffered and too cocooned or rigidly remain in our own linguistic bubble we will not connect, we will not grow. And the rich offerings that a new language provides will pass us by. That contact should be direct, personal and immediate. If confronting new people, other lifestyles and a language that is not your own, is filtered through the eyes and reactions of someone else, they become diluted and diminished. That whole other commentary will stand between you and immersion, obstructing your cultural and linguistic goal.

I am enjoying eavesdropping on these women and their exchanges in English though I know I shouldn't, and I am intrigued at their interactions – at a professional level, since it is hard to resist the urge – I relish the technical skill of the group leader, how she teases out and establishes an exchange between people who clearly don't know one another. In particular I pick up on her explanation regarding linguistic and grammatical difference in how French and English relay the same concept. 'In French we have age,' she says, 'whereas in English we are age.' I begin to reflect on the notion that in the UK where English is our native language, age defines us. Whereas in France apparently, age is seen as an external, we own it, possess it but it is not intrinsic to who we are. It is in fact 'just a number'!

Language is very much framed by its surrounding and historical culture, the product of a certain philosophy, outlook and value system and it is key to how we perceive the world. Different languages represent different perspectives or provide a different focus and current studies suggest that bilingualism and multilingualism, as well as the reading of translated literature generally, bring us an ability to see things from various vantage points, thus broadening our world view and increasing our creative flow. In the toing and froing across that linguistic and cultural divide and the ability to adopt very different mindsets, we expand who we are.

There have been a few times, when I have had a conversation with someone, when we have used the

*Every social interaction... has the potential
for both cultural persistence and change.*

(Ochs, 1996)

same words, defined our terms of reference even, and to
all intents and purposes are communicating very well.
But I have often found that that may not necessarily
be so. We may have adopted a common vocabulary,
similar registers of formality, intimacy or light-hearted
sociability, but the content of our words might be totally
different depending on our respective mental make-
up, our histories, how our minds work and what our
intention is.

Our voiced words are only indicators of our
openness, and willingness to engage. They are quite
simply the platform on which we communicate; through
what is spoken and unspoken we interconnect or co-
operate towards a common goal. That dialogue between
two people can open up a creative space for shift and
respective self-production or change. Through common
endeavour each acquires fresh ways of seeing the world;
curiosity and adventure play their hand. We might enrol
in an evening class in phonetics, write a novella, join a
chorus or start hugging trees.

In coming face-to-face with those new ideas,
perspectives and practices that a language presents when
it is not our own, change may come in unexpected ways
and the potential for other enactments of ourselves in
entirely unprecedented, individualistic ways and non-
normative ways. An engagement with otherness by

means of total linguistic immersion can be a catalyst in our continued story of construction and rebuilding of the self. Briefly, as we delve deeper and more extensively into other languages, the more choice, opportunity, variability and flexibility is at our disposal. The more fragile, flimsy, volatile and even contradictory the self becomes.

In Italy, who I am depends on whether I am in Milan, Florence or the hills of the Abbruzzi. What I laugh at in Cassino, may not be the same as things that amuse me in Pisa. What I want to eat in Sardinia is not what I feel like eating in Rome. The person that walked those lovely streets past that fine Cathédrale de Saint Sauveur with its 5th century baptismal font is not the person that walked along the Faubourg St Honoré in Paris last October and stopped to have a *salade niçoise*. In France's magnificent south, I feel the need to breakfast on a thick slice of sourdough with butter and jam whereas in Paris, nothing other than a croissant will do. In Spain, I would never dream of corn flakes or a digestive biscuit but only *pan con tomate* with a fair helping of salt. In Greece I follow the pies or the yoghurt. None of these identities are the same as that of the person huddling in a sleeping bag or eating a scone in a latte joint. It is the language and all that is contained in that language, together with its regional and dialectical idiosyncrasies that makes different requirements and creates diverse and varied, often unprecedented personal upheaval.

A monolingual society is by definition closed off, circumscribed and excluded from this abundance of possibility, opportunity and personal choice. There is no halo or benefit in monolingualism. Much is to be gained by plurilanguaging. Long may we encourage the learning of a multiplicity of languages and the nation's openness to that abundance of treasures. Long may we do our utmost to encourage and facilitate exposure for people at all ages and in particular, for the very young, to all that emerges from the skills, intellects and artistry of a global world, in which every country though culturally and linguistically distinct and proud, at the same time uniquely connects in spirit and seeks out its neighbours above and beyond any national borders.

I left France a few weeks ago. My language is not what it was once. I needed longer. But when a man I had been speaking to in the queue for flight check-in asked me why as a Frenchwoman I was living in Edinburgh, when FNAC sends me updates about new French publications and Black Friday deals and when Google starts speaking to me in French, I feel those six weeks brought back a self long set aside, and someone that those around me may have some problems getting to grips with. For a glorious short time at least.

shift

... it was a school in the central belt and there was the usual flurry at the start of the day, when classes are about to begin; teachers and students hover and bustle, general movement in and out of classroom doors, hurried exchanges, bags and papers; and Inspectors (appointed in the service of Her Majesty no less) gather in a 'base room', dedicated for the inspection period, to accommodate the team and quiet working. I have some fond memories of these oases, in colleges and schools up and down the country: days of dejection, of dispute, anxiety and self-doubt, of drama and of wonderful stories, rich with wit and laughter, days of colleagues' support in the face of fierce, adversarial opposition from those being inspected and days when I had to stick to my convictions in a sometimes unconvinced team, unwilling to budge from my evaluations because of the clear messages from both evidence and the second, more instinctive brain in my gut.

But I remember this particular morning very clearly. The dinner ladies, who particularly tended to spoil the menfolk of the team, always piling plates high in school dining rooms, brought the usual pile of chocolate traybakes and left them in the corner of the room near the electric kettle. It was day four of the five day school inspection and each day, I had with huge effort, resisted temptation. Everyone left to go and observe classes. Suddenly, all was quiet, learning and process underway, the building now hushed, I was alone and I had some time available before I was due to start reviewing evidence and prepare for the coming day. So, notes and laptop in front of me, I sat instead, staring at the cakes... the soft, rich chocolate, dark fruit breaking the surface... and I began to salivate. Try as I might, I was unable to put them out of my mind and concentrate like a responsible adult on the serious business at hand, the data, the statements, the evaluation criteria. Then, suddenly, like a bird of prey, as if devil possessed, I swooped... one, two, three and then a fourth. I gobbled them up – in the true sense of the French word *avaler* – and quickly (just in case I might be caught in the act, fully suited, crisp white shirt, loitering over the wonderful, sweet delights, chocolate all over hands and face). Explain it? Impossible!

This journey of education, my firm and lifelong dedication to it, I cannot say less, and not indeed to cakes usually, began in a small kitchen, the distant sound of *Corrie* or maybe *Take Your Pick,* that old quiz show, from the sitting room where my grandmother was. I had been sitting at the wooden table in the kitchen recess. I had just finished my homework. I was nine years old. I am going to be a teacher I thought, that's what I want to do. At university, I was one of eight students in the Italian Honours programme and one of 500 in the French programme. I came through strongly in the latter, achieving more than the required 65 per cent at first sitting of exams. This qualified me and around 40 others for Junior Honours. The Italian department was however, dominated by a strong Oxbridge ethos and I was one of two somewhat disenfranchised Scottish students; we were cultural outsiders. The sherry parties, visiting professors, at-homes in sleek Swedish-styled dwellings with vases of flowers; the smooth-toned, lengthy and self-consciously, erudite delivery in tutorials by both tutors and students, the confident air of everyone around reduced me to either silence, to tongue-tied incoherence when I did summon any courage to speak or to abject, monosyllabic utterances. All of these academic and social niceties were completely bewildering to a girl from a disordered, disinhibited Italian home with a narrow, celibate convent upbringing. I did not feel and was neither seen as, it seemed to me, worthy of this sophisticated, elite, glossy 'packaging'; nor did I have a place in these alien conditions of existence... I was altogether too unstyled and too direct.

When my professor looked at me, I thought I saw a trace of sadness or disappointment in his eyes which he tried to mask by an over-charming smile and which he maybe hoped might mitigate or wipe out any lack of refinement, any blunderingly embarrassing behaviour, on my part. He was neither impressed by me nor aspirational for me. I was, I should add, a fluent, authentic speaker and an avid student of the medievalists. He saw none of it. Indeed my Italian accent was a good bit better than his. He could neither tune into the cadence of Italian nor desist from plum English vowel bending. I was also the first languages student to embark on a new Joint Honours languages degree at Edinburgh University. The day by day impact of these rather unhappy encounters and the low expectations around me, hovering at every assignment and walking with me into every lecture room, led me ultimately to stand aside and build from inside; to look for reassurance instead from what was inside me, to assess what and how much I knew for myself; had processed and engaged with. I adopted my own independent course of somehow wider, off-syllabus learning. Some of this was to achieve the degree, but for the most part, my aim was to live a productive and fruitful other life at the same time, benefiting from the more solid education of whizzing around France on a moped and sharing a flat with French students. None of this was at all relevant to achieving a formal qualification but very relevant to my own self-making and identity building.

The other effect of this continual put down was to make me resolute. So, rather than depress my energy for self-making, it fed it; the injustice I sensed stoked only determined fury. There is a great validity in this approach I discovered, much later in life, when I came out of retirement to work as a part-time lecturer at a university in the West of Scotland preparing adults of all ages for their return to education and a full-time degree course. My approach to this was to validate the skills they had acquired through life experience – parenthood, career, travel, home management – and convince them of their relevance to full-time study and student life.

The other cornerstone for my career decisions became ever more solid as I undertook training to qualify as a teacher. Released from the pressure of having to battle constantly for some kind of validation, in this subsequent diploma course of preparation for teaching and in the classroom, I was seen as a natural, at ease with young people. I took easily to it and I did very well. I was, university behind me, now well positioned and I strode forward with long confident steps, determined to show what I was really made of, to be the best, to excel, and I started to map my optimum career route towards educational leadership.

As a classroom teacher, indeed as an inspector too of schools and adult learning, I did not have a lot of time for the tokenism and drudgery of homework. I could appreciate the discipline of it, the inculcation of good habits, a good work ethic. But for me, it seemed, certainly as an exercise for the youngest secondary school learners, to be a very arid, cold, mechanical exercise, voided of the voice or personality which is the tender trap of education: the compelling call which brings you back and back. Homework is rather akin to what is left of fruit after the sheer pleasure of consuming its sweet flesh is over, the desiccated husk of a live encounter.

The contrary approach, that of 'flipping classrooms' (a learning strategy which is used successfully mainly in Higher Education) where learning is what takes place in the home, in one's own time, outside of school through internet and libraries, and the reversed role of a classroom, where learners bring knowledge to be discussed with an 'expert' (the teacher) on hand, rather than receiving or being filled up, rather like a thermos flask, with knowledge, seems to me to make more sense. This teaching method has shown itself to allow for more differentiated learning focusing on the requirements of each individual. That said, I am more than conscious that for many, many young people, circumstances make home study impossible and even after-school homework drop-ins, are not always favourable in relation to their other life demands; many young people only just manage to make it to the school door and to get through the day despite what is going on at home. Sometimes to just survive what is around them even at school, in toilet blocks, classrooms and playground is even more challenging. I know this from my own experience, trying to hold a steady line, ears clamped shut, with the comings and goings of extended family, the showdowns and shoot outs of uncles and cousins and the buzz of exchanges about shop life, all circling me as I sat alone on my island, the kitchen table, soon needed for a meal or for cups of tea and family chat.

Unlike many of my young learners, there was a lot of encouragement at home for my school commitments. How do young people survive? How do they cope in neighbourhoods where you are either the victim, or in order to stay alive, forced to be the mean aggressor; where you try to walk with your head down when you go to the shops fearful that even that lack of eye contact may provoke an attack. What do we know of it? Darren McGarvey in *Poverty Safari* tells it plainly; yes, he opens our eyes, we who teach, who govern and legislate, we whose job and prime obligation it is to know precisely what kind of lives our young people live, what they contend with, so that we can teach better, educate with wisdom and communicate more smartly: 'so this is how people dress when they aren't afraid of being stabbed', he writes about the Glasgow West End coffee gurus lolling in the boutiques and bars, those *fika* spaces and *anticafés* of Byres Road.

While reading for my thesis I came across a fascinating literature about power relations within schools, and the clash of values in a classroom environment. Bourdieu in *Reproduction in Education, Society and Culture* (Bourdieu and Passeron, 1977) describes education as a means of transmitting bourgeois-led ideologies, aspirations and a certain lifestyle, and imposing a culture on many learners which is alien to them. How learning is organised, designed and delivered and the fundamental beliefs and lifestyles of those delivering education are founded on middle class values and ideology which favours some and disfavours others.

In this context, certain educational goals, aspirations and behaviours carry status thus marginalising some learners who are already socially disadvantaged and encouraging others who are already better positioned. Other writers, Foucault (1995), Sarup (1982) have described schools in terms of social control, hierarchy and places of ideological pressure. I have always been conscious of a class system or class bias inherent within the very foundations and structure of educational provision, of standards, expectations and behaviours.

Education in all its facets is generally a middle class preserve, meeting best the needs of the private sector and feeding a capitalist economy. While those who set the educational agenda speak eloquently of social disadvantage and the attainment gap, while they are aware that not all students come to education ready, free or able to fully enter into the conversation or the work at hand, somehow nonetheless, those difficult, painful and sometimes even insurmountable barriers are neither sufficiently addressed or radically removed.

For me, the purpose of education is surely to enable each individual to grow and develop, to provide skills that will always take her forward in whatever direction she chooses. A strong economy is built through a society where both the weak and the strong are catered for and as well-equipped individuals, are well positioned make the best contribution possible.

What do we make of the terms 'excellent', 'outstanding' and the current 'edubabble' of the education world, of the commodification of education, the marketing industries around it, the large gross banners sprawled on school gates, like posters for a West End show, and the media hullabaloo around national standards, schools' performance and league tables. Some multi-academy trusts in England and Wales have criticised OFSTED, the regulator of schools south of the border describing it as a middle class framework for middle class children. OFSTED on the other hand reports that the most disadvantaged children are being seriously let down by a narrow curriculum and a more limited choice than the more able. How do they fit, these unreal expectations and far out claims with the stark situation of a struggling 16-year-old, who can never be excellent when it is all he can do to stay breathing each day, who is constantly poised on the thin, narrow ridges of existence, and where, at any moment, the complete abyss that yawns at his feet might just swallow him whole.

My three years of service with the Children's Hearing System in Scotland taught me this. Having worked in the state sector for many years, I thought I knew something about social deprivation. I realised that I knew nothing. But I met more than a few young people who were at severe risk of suicide, who had made several attempts, and who were under close scrutiny. My experience thankfully, also taught me that miracles do happen and that now and again, a young person emerges from that dark room, with peeling wallpaper and bare boards sodden with the detritus of life, with a strengthened inner core and a bright eye to what lies beyond and where there has somehow, magically, been a turning point. 'At a time in my life when I needed it, you said that you believed I could do it,' she told me. She was now a senior executive in Scottish Enterprise; she had been in my fourth year French class when she was 15 years old.

And as a member of the Children's Panel, I met a boy called Bobby before the tribunal convened to review his case. He was with his social worker and was in Care. His grades at school were very good, he was about to start an internship, was smiling, relaxed and tidy. While maintaining his family ties, he had moved his life on. He had plans and a bright future. These survivors exist. They are the lucky few maybe. But survival and thriving are almost always possible. At a young age they have crawled out from under, from a system that does not get it or them because the gulf is too great, the instruments too blunt and the investment just not enough.

I also learned something else from that three-year Panel service and all the years before. Teachers are professional learners. That is our métier, to learn. And through learning, with open minds, we improve as communicators, as relators, as team players and as creators. And we learn mainly from those we teach. They tell us what they need if we allow them to and if we are quiet enough to hear them, for often there is too little space for them to speak. And they also require more than a little respect from us for what they, and not we, know about life. For it just might be that they know a bit more than we do: offer a different kind of knowledge and another perspective or reflection on life experiences. Let us acknowledge that we as professionals and experts have things to impart; but that equally, there is much that our young folk can teach us.

The trick of education for the sake of engagement and take-up, is to match or frame surely, what is to be learned to the lived experience of those we teach. It is not to conjure up, like a rabbit out of a hat, a way of thinking or life goals as alien to our students as a time-travelling machine from outer space. I still remember having to teach children learning French the words for Madame Marsaud who was always preoccupied chapter by chapter, with vacuum cleaning the house and doing the dishes; a Monsieur Marsaud perpetually in the garden. I wonder now how meaningful, or indeed useful, such a shamelessly classist, gendered curriculum was to kids from the louche, dark tenements of central Edinburgh.

One of the truest statements I have read about Education is that a learning space should be hospitable. I believe this to be so in every sense of that word. The polemic and literature around 'hospitable spaces' comes from a distinctive theology and religious mission I gather. But what a difference it would make if every teacher were sufficiently resourced, supported and valued, by an education policy and funding regime that truly understands and values the process. If that policy were to embody the notion that real engagement with learning and the true path to attainment comes from a face-to-face dynamic. If it defined learning as a gut connection, a message passed from person to person, sometimes unvoiced, a transaction, a transmission of belief, conviction, energy and enthusiasm between people.

If too, every classroom were a welcoming place of safety for both learners and teachers, a place of acceptance, where every individual feels valued and has her place, where it's okay to fall flat on your face, to look silly; where what you bring and all that you offer is respected; where your successes are celebrated and where talent is nurtured. Most surely, personal achievement and success would emerge strongly. It would grow and flow most naturally and abundantly. And what a glorious gift, what a lifeline that would be for every child irrespective of what they have witnessed, grown up with or left behind them at home. The imposition of hard targets with meaningless labels and straplines, the decanting of large numbers of children into classes where individuals disappear into the masses and teaching becomes didactic, a repetitive mind-numbing endurance test; and a compliance model instead of a collaborative, inclusive and exciting joint venture, is neither inspiring, nor educational. It is ultimately downright unsuccessful.

Most importantly, this value clash, the daily battles between contradictory ideologies fought in classrooms every day up and down the land, leaves young people already living on the hard edges of our communities even further disenfranchised and frustrated by their seeming worthlessness in a bewildering world and within a system that is for others and not for them. There is constant national interest around 'closing the educational gap' for young people who either give up on school or leave with poor grades, are unemployable and revert to living the life they have seen, grew up with and come to expect, a life of benefits, dependency and hopelessness. The transformative potential and power of education is indisputable, is awesome. The miracles are within reach for everyone. All that is required is vision, resources, creativity and professional belief in and commitment to its magic.

propulsion

'... I just don't know if there will ever gonna be a time when I'm gonna ever really find the real me because I'm always goin' aboot open tae other things and as long as I leave masel open tae experience, how can a be the real me because I'm gonna be learning and takin' on mair knowledge...'

... at the start of a doctoral programme which I committed to in my mid-50s, we were warned: 'This experience will alter your lives in ways that you do not maybe want or expect. It will disrupt, challenge, lead to broken relationships, lose you friends.' And so, mid-career, with grudging encouragement and some perhaps, surprise from a few quarters, I reduced my income significantly, reduced my working hours by half, compromised the golden handshake of a comfortable civil service pension and embarked on a major life journey towards a doctorate.

My research involved a number of volunteer participants, mainly adults at college with few or no qualifications. I wanted to explore the impact of new learning, learn from it myself and most importantly, share the outcomes. I met Marie first. She was in her 40s. She was reserved and spoke in a very quiet, even tone. I found her difficult to read and I was initially unable to form any strong impression but it seemed to me that she had a story to tell and that despite the painful memory that the telling of her story would cause her, she was determined for whatever reason, to proceed. She smiled a great deal but there was no joy or laughter there, only a sad acceptance. Nor was she over-anxious to connect with me.

We had very little eye contact. It was as though in telling me her story, she was at times, going through a ritual, at others, she had to look deep within her to summon all her resources to do what she had set out to do. And therefore my reactions mattered very little and I was totally unprepared for her revelations.

She had been adopted by a devoutly, religious couple at an early age. At a certain point in her growing up, her father turned his sexual attentions on her. A regular weekly practice ensued and continued for some years. Every Thursday when her mother went out, he visited her room and abused her.

She spoke with pain about the minutes after he left the room; of turning to face the wall. She spoke about hearing the front door close when her mother left the house. At the end of our second discussion, she gave me some of her poems to read, describing her feelings and in one, begging her mother not to go out that night.

After the death of first her father, and years after her mother, she realised how much she had lived her life around her parents needs and wishes, protecting them at her own expense. Looking at her dead mother, lying on the floor 'with her eyes open' all she felt she said, was anger and she described the temptation not to help her father as he was dying of a stroke was almost impossible to overcome. Almost middle-aged now, in her own words, she was still looking for Marie, trying to 'find herself'.

She described her new life with positivity and as one of self-direction and journey: 'You are in a darkened room, and the curtain's black and there's a wee, tiny, tiny, tiny hole in it and you can see the sun shining through it and it doesn't matter about all that blackness around you, you'll focus on that tiny, tiny wee light.' It might have seemed that nothing can bring you back from that. The guilt, the vacuum within, the compromised loyalties, the destructiveness and devastation of her situation, her powerlessness and the awareness of her own power to stop it but she didn't, lasted many long years. Yet somehow she had been able still, to see just a little light.

Through all the wonders of valuing relationships in that new space of learning, through all the intimacies exchanged between herself and those good folk around her, all the voiced and unvoiced dialogues, all the empathy, understandings, friendship, sense of worthiness that others gave her, she was enabled enough to follow that chink of light until it grew larger and more intense. She followed it until she became able, until she became another, new, increasingly fulfilled woman and the woman sitting in front of me, now stilled, tranquil and day-on-day more buoyant and hope-filled about her future, and what her life now beginning, might be.

There were many others, seeking to overturn the past events of their lives or to change their circumstances; to change who they had allowed themselves to become. Carrie was in her 40s too; her goal was to be a teacher, and she had come back to education in order to gain the necessary qualifications for a degree course at a university. She had finally freed herself from the festering wounds of her background, from her mother, her mother's alcoholism, a bullying home environment; and because of her mother, a childhood of isolation and distance from her peers. She had turned her back on a mapped out identity rooted in established norms and the old ways of a certain Scottish community and a fixed, rigid mentality, had recreated her identity, changed who she was and how she appeared, in the world. Through her children, her marriage, her independence and her friends she had styled herself differently, remoulded herself as a prospective professional about to become a teacher. She was not 'lucky' she said. She had made thoughtful choices.

Mary was an escapee from a destructive marriage and an alcoholic husband whose extreme behaviour had terrorised her and increasingly her eight-year-old daughter who was at risk of harm on a daily basis. Her lack of formal education, her problems with basic literacy, did not phase her and neither was it a problem in her college programme. It was accounted for and could be addressed. Finally, strong and positive, she had developed focus and determination.

Annie had been brought up in a Scottish mining community and had interrupted her studies at school in order to care for her father until he died. She eventually fell in love and lived with her partner for many years. His gambling addiction increasingly took hold however. They separated and his subsequent, sudden death, followed by her own breakdown, led her ultimately to enrol in a full-time college programme.

As weeks went by, the daily life patterns of these individuals and of the other adult learners that I met, from a variety of programmes, how they saw themselves, their manner of speaking, the language they used, all began to change. In a fairly short time frame, I was party to their slow, steady building of self-belief, of confidence, ambition and aspiration. They seemed more in control, with a strong sense of their own power. The despair that they had arrived with had receded. And they had arrived at a view of their past, now behind them, which enabled them to move forward. Each one had set out seeking a qualification, enrolling in a course that might lead to employment and possibly a new life. But it was the totality of the experience, the nurturing, wholesome, validating weekly environment of the classroom and those around them which was gradually having a profound impact. Fellow learners, lecturers, mentors and supervisors were all playing their part in a truly transformational life event.

These individuals had survived so much, showed increasing bravery and I saw human resolve and courage together with talent, energy and positivity. As they spoke, I could see their vision of a fresh future; a vision which had somehow grown from what little had been left of them.

Like many people whose need is too great to bear, who live in what seems like a wilderness, something had broken, given way to something altogether more powerful which had flooded in. The energy and force of it had been irresistible, leaving them unable to do other than to follow. Drained, utterly weakened and weary, with no further down that deep dark well to go, repelled ultimately by the entrapment of it, disappointed at themselves too for years of not confronting their situation, a sudden force within them had sprung up. Ultimately freed, shackles cast aside, and now supported in another environment, they stood easily, exuberantly, triumphantly on the threshold of a new life and a new identity.

From both a personal and a professional standpoint, I see learning as escape, as renewal, as a steadying, as a means of continually creating. It is from that sustaining platform that we can find resolution, understand better, seek adventure and look to what else there might be. Learning has ultimately always been an intimate matter for me. My faith in education as uniquely transformative, able to release potential that you didn't even know that you had, to making you the person that you never imagined, is unshakeable. And the many students and young people that I have met professionally have also been part of my own journey of change, future and possibility as we travelled the same road together, though having started out very differently.

If only among other much needed social change and reorganisation, we could in first-chance education, in school and even in pre-school provision, find the kind of approaches, the kind of language, gut feel and understandings; a quality of relating that works for the majority. How different, how changed and how so eminently fulfilled lives and futures could be, how buoyant an economy, how contented a workforce, how equal a society, throughout a Scotland – as I write – seeking its own distinctive and independent future.

We can always be the victim. We can often fall into accepting, resigned to leading our lives as prisoners of another individual, of a poor education, of a family or community, of a life or conditions that we feel others impose. There are of course too, often rigid, historic and unassailable structural barriers: the prison gates of the way society is ordered, the political colours, directions, impasses and failures; the unwillingness of a boss, an interview panel, a society and its transient values, its obsessions, scapegoating and discriminations that vary and or pass, becoming more and more extreme from generation to generation.

These factors and a host of others are the obstructions to ultimately seeing you in all your glory, accepting you in your fullness, to making your way easier, bringing you on and developing you; to believing in you, to loving you. A way forward is always possible for at least some of us, if not many. Our minds, the good experiences we have, what we focus on, the more positive and uplifting the better, can strengthen those neural pathways in the brain.

To the bullies at work who almost gave me a breakdown, thank you, I am the better; to those men with no other entitlement or achievement but their penis – maybe a flash suit – and who hacked away at my confidence, thank you, I am the stronger; to the teachers whose favourite I was not, the friends and associates who thrived on gossip, I bless you all. Through you all, I developed steel, I took the journeys, and the will and worth that you tried to break, for whatever reason, morphed into pride that grew in darkness and that I hot housed like fragile saplings. It was a long game, cultivated in response, and you never, not even once saw the distress you caused. Because for you all, most especially, and for the world too, I made it look effortless. That was intentional. And to the individuals that really saw me, to those warriors that inspired me, those Joans of Arc, Angelous and the rest, I thank you for the inspiration and the will to go on.

For the sake of your precious life, let the pain and turmoil which that god awful, that bile inducing obduracy and blindness arouses in you, let the frustration, simmering anger or anguish that these injustices cause, be the catalyst. Seek out instead the power givers, whatever that or they may be. Give no quarter. If there are buts and maybes do not listen. If there are tears, question why. Hike on and up and away. Let Education, role models, inspiring quotes, books, philosophies, religions even, and your very own mind and energies, rouse you and give you fire. Above all seek odes of glory and triumph. Follow the stories of Bader Ginsberg, the first Jewish woman to serve on the US Supreme Court, Patrisse Cullors of BLM distinction and so many others. Seek the glass, the steel and soaring heights, seek the promise of city lights as the sun goes down... as you glimpse for a first time, the nightime aura of Rio or Paris from an airplane window; gaze childlike at buildings that sit bright and ride on surf, at mountain tops that splinter sunlight; make time for words of great and lesser poets; pause at a baby's babbling, at a hat taken by the wind, at acoustic guitar riffs, at syncopation. Enjoy, enjoy, enjoy. For that simple joy is your birthright.

wordscaping

...where yesterday the bright earth explodes, brim-full and bulging, reaches up on tiptoes to sunshine; where it dips and tumbles into the fullness of sun's close embrace. Today, the same ground flattens to a thin, black line, retreating into itself and hardening its fragile crust, summoning all its resources in order to withstand the slow, steady imposition of mist on its filmy membrane, its insistent, creeping advance, drop by drop and layer by layer, into every private creek and unseen curve.

Barra, where the fog was so dense on a day last summer, I was virtually blinded, sucked into its damp veiling, it was all I could do to breathe; though much less. It seemed to me that the air was choked with moisture, soaking through all the available oxygen. Reminding me of the fullness of night when my world is smaller, when there is only as far as I can feel and touch and everything has retired to where it sleeps and takes its rest. These are the times when I am at my most immediate and free; reminding me that these are the best times to write.

It is often true that the final pronouncements on a relationship which is ending sometimes produce an initial momentary lightness, euphoria even, of returning to yourself and your uncompromised, unimpeachable wholeness! Then the rest follows and follows and doggedly follows. The sense of skin ripped away, your raw rancid flesh, shivering, bleeding at every frisson: every look in your direction, any whiff of coolness, tenderness, even laugher which comes from another table; every touch of one hand on another that makes you push away your plate of food, switch off your phone and stay in bed for the day; and if someone lovingly touches yours, you begin to tremble, your mouth dries up, tears gather, drop steadily – and you might or might not vomit. Your stomach has been wrenched from your belly, there's a pulsating black hole in its place, a void that spreads to your throat, tightening its grip, makes you hoarse, while bile, wherever you are and whatever you're doing, is your faithful friend. And you might even glimpse a spider, or two maybe, with fangs and four rotating eyes; or imagine that you do, somewhere in the gloom; the gloom that you struggle with as it slams you in the face every morning on first waking and that you try to surface from, like a swimmer thrashing about, trying not to surrender, not to lose your hold on sensible life, in a deep black sea.

I was working as a volunteer at the Centre for World Peace on Holy Isle one winter some years ago. A sack of potatoes, or three buckets of basil to process in order to make pesto are good therapy for what they call a broken heart. I was at a point in my life when, with several broken relationships behind me, there seemed to be nothing for it but to start again. The island's grass and mud underfoot had received me warmly when I got off the boat and when I stood in the small corridor of the main house, and removed my shoes to go upstairs, the bricks and mortar, warm and seasoned with the aspirations, fresh healing and love of those who had passed through or lingered here maybe only to offer a silent, tear filled embrace, closed in around me and held me tight: 'you will be okay' they seemed to say, 'you can rest here'. Then in my simple room, a very familiar room, with a window view of only bush and trees and damp leaves in the fading afternoon light, there was no world to contend with anymore. It was gone. And with its vanishing, its complexities too: the requirements, the constructions, the questioning, the masking and unmasking, the navigating and appeasing, the importance – duty even – of keeping things on track; the endless demands that however you feel, you must keep on spinning those wheels in your time-limited slot.

In that reduced, spare universe of only a bed, a table, somewhere to hang my clothes, I sat and looked around, and I suddenly saw in large relief, a quite broken but nonetheless solid, me. Questions might be asked; eyebrows raised; judgements meted out, recorded, talked about. People can misunderstand and misconstrue, make a story from a word. They can like, love, or however hard you try, coldly dislike you or even worse, pretend to be your friend.

But suddenly I filled the room, this me, that I saw that evening, and, however things turn out or appear, this me does her best. I am well-intentioned; I get weary, angry. I can also be passionate, loving, inspired and inspiring, happy and joyful. I have hurt and failed people, been hurt and failed in return – and I have loved and been loved in equal measure. This me, whatever and whoever I am, is, in the end, all I can rely on. I can make or do; I can build and rebuild. I can always start again, come back to the start line. This me is the source, and the one and only source, of all that my life is and can still be. I learned then, in the smallness and the silence of that space, my physical presence substantial within it, that it is only in coming back to self, in discarding all the trappings and ultimately irrelevances that we crowd our lives with, that we can do something meaningful, that we can turn things around.

So, in the following days, standing at the sink or among a pile of cabbages to be washed and chopped, from what I knew I could do reliably, those practical things, and from within the old loose T-shirt, baggy jeans, the overalls of kitchen hand and a mind blanked, that wanted neither to evaluate, to reflect or consider, from behind the faking, the Arlecchino showy grin, out of the settling pile of debris within, emerged, slowly at first, something fragile and tenuous but a fine-spun line nonetheless, that could take me forward. I greeted the shy smile that spread, took over and strengthened my days.

Around 6.00am one morning, in a freezing, empty dining room, with no forethought, no grand plan, I switched on the light, sat at a window facing blackness, where the sea usually was, and I wrote two poems rapidly, for that is how they came. They were not love poems and not my first, but they were the first for almost four decades. The first after my adolescent preoccupations of romance, death etc. and a tentative foray or return to my quieter world of before.

The first poem, which was not really a poem at all, was a kind of evocation of a fractured self, a jigsaw, with nothing to hold the pieces together. Except that the pieces did all fit. They were joined together, and each played their full part in the whole piece. After that morning, in these eight years that have followed, I have written and written, as if in a frenzy, as if something had broken apart within me, a spirit let loose that would not be silenced; and with every poem, book, or article, although more paced now, I am on a journey. I have an objective.

Throughout my life, I have been an avid reader and I have been privileged to pick up (often randomly), to discover and enjoy some of the best writers from wonderful literary traditions beyond English – the writing from France and Italy and elsewhere. I am not a lover of biography or life history writing, I never sought that kind of writing, but over a three year period, with strong recommendations, I made a happy and satisfying incursion into Elena Ferrante's writing (which is, I am sure, at least in part if not entirely autobiographical I'm sure); and the entire six volume masterpiece, *My Struggle* by Karl Ove Knausgård, including his 11,000 page conclusion, which I swallowed whole without so much as a quick read at a daily news round-up, during a summer in Scotland's best scenery. I was spellbound by both.

More recently, I have increasingly turned to Eastern writers, such as Khaled Hosseini's *A Thousand Splendid Suns* and, sought out women writers of fiction who have grown up in the Muslim tradition; or indeed male writers who challenge what we in the West regard as repressive norms and religious imposition on women and men. The most memorable of these have been Ece Temelkuran's *Women Who Blow on Knots*, Elif Shafak's *The Bastard of Istanbul* and *Three Daughters of Eve*; and *Guapa* by Saleem Haddad. *Season of Crimson Blossoms* by Abubakar Adam Ibrahim also

made a huge impression on me. That reading history –
of French Romanticism and Existentialism (the abstract
and the philosophising), the rationalist ideas of the
Enlightenment, the concrete in the Italian medievalists,
the Futurists and the post-Risorgimento writers such
as Pirandello and Svevo, explorations of reality and
unreality and the emergence of a literature in the Italian
vernacular; of Asian feminism and protest – has all not
surprisingly, had a huge impact on my own writing,
my aspirations and ideals, on what I value and my own
writing goals.

Somehow in the counterflow however, and contrary
to current trends in poetry and prose writing, my
literary interests, my own ideals lie in durability, a
certain sense of worthiness and I am utterly seduced
by evocative language and its music. Gabriel García
Márquez must surely fit that entire bill. I believe as
writers, however we write, convincingly, artfully,
beautifully, brutally, and never as well as we would
like, we owe it to those greats before us, to honour
their fine legacy of commentary, confrontation, satire,
humour, beauty, escapism and above all inspiration to
list only some of their gifts to history and to humanity.

As a reader, what elates me, brings me joy, takes
me to another level beyond the everyday concerns
and practicalities, is an aesthetic, an intoxicating mix,
of reality imbued with emotion, brought into being
through words, harmony, a brush stroke, poster or a
fishing net. In our everyday lives, we are bombarded
with fiction – on our browsers, in our junk mail, on
Instagram, Twitter and Facebook, where as a society
we present the versions of ourselves we want the world
to see.

I don't write a book so that it will be the final word; I write a book so that other books are possible, not necessarily written by me. (Foucault)

We hear fiction every day from politicians who legitimately lie and are admired for their 'balls' and in some cases, blatant moral decrepitude. We emulate or are intrigued by larger than life public figures in the media. We feel diminished by or compete with the well-glossed and painted avatars, carefully crafted images of unreality, roaming in cocktail and coffee bars, night clubs and we frequent art galleries and concert halls, where to understand what you see or hear, you are obliged to digest a few pages of A5 obscure material first. We need fairy stories of course, for they once told us and we grew to believe that the world is made up of good things and all will be well. We need fiction that connects with our experience as human beings for it is better to know that you are not alone with your feelings and your destiny and that all is at least normal and maybe even salvageable. We need tales of hope, that promise justice and reassure us of the good nature in our fellow humans. Fiction's gift to us.

We also need a literature that brings out the best in us, the showstoppers that open our eyes. But for the present time, I am not a storyteller and I have chosen a different route with the intention always to communicate, for that is surely why we write. From those first steps on Holy Isle, from that kitchen and those first poems, the literature of a lifetime returned to me, all the writing that I had loved and admired urged me on – the writing of reports and papers to inform, encourage and persuade colleagues – to offer a vision, to set parameters, to interpret, published and unpublished, stood at my back and I wrote my first book, a personal story, a memoir with a message.

Language of My Choosing (Luath Press, 2017), later published in translation in Italy in 2018, was an amazing experience of excitement, fulfilment and challenge. There was never any plan to write a book and here I am now, writing another. I wrote *Language* in response to a dare from a good friend to whom I had sent some poems for a view. I am very grateful to Luath Press for its steady faith in me. A new writer is risky. The making of the book led me of course to reflect a great deal; it led to a deeper understanding of myself and an appraisal of my life; it forced me to look at myself from the objectivity of a reader and to wrestle at times with an honest acceptance and admission of the person, indeed persons that I am. I discovered feelings that I had never dared to acknowledge: for the first time I saw value in the actions of some of the people in my past where before I had condemned them – some became elevated to saintliness and the heroic almost. I recognised motives and impulses in myself and others, forces at work which I could never have countered far less defeated, only managed.

Most importantly, having at times in my life been critical of my mother and her mothering of me, as I wrote, I grew to see things from a different perspective. With that growing recognition of her as a woman, I became reconciled with her, saw her efforts to do the best she could for me in her own way and having lived a life, as a mother myself, I became sympathetic to what drove her in a way I had not before. This was ultimately a redemptive journey of forgiveness, absolution and a letting go of guilt, a recognition of what it is to be human, to both fail and to succeed. In the end, through writing the book, I became reconciled with myself. I became grateful for my luck in life and proud of what had been passed on. I grew with the book and with its aftermath. There was never any guarantee of publication. I remained unsure of the outcome but having started, it seemed that the book was already inside me. It was only a question of writing it down in a way that would best share my journey.

I am an obsessive writer, meaning that once started, I will not let go. It has me in its grip. Having cleared out the emotional debris of years, rogue thoughts and firm convictions that had littered my mind, threaded their way in and out of my life for such a long time, I find now that as a writer of poetry, I hesitate to call myself a poet, I work in two ways. I am either open to a new subject, I put myself in the way of something I might want to write about and something that could capture my interest. In which case I stalk, I linger, I watch and listen. I attend creative writing workshops led by professionals in and around the city and I usually come away with something I can work on.

Or, I become completely buried in something, an idea, an event which has caught my fancy, which has caused me some turmoil, led to an emotional outburst or reaction. In the case of the latter, I like to combine my writing of the poems with some research too and I am a frequent visitor to libraries wherever I find myself. I have worked in libraries from Lewisham to Aix-en-Provence to Mallaig, frequently in London in The British

Library and very often among the young, rich and stylish in the library of the University of Edinburgh. (Whatever happened to that old frame bed and the *vecchia zimarra* of Bohème and those I knew in my time at university I wonder?)

The harder I try to find the words or write the lines, the more obstinate and unwilling my mind becomes and the less I can write; and only when I am relaxed and a little lighter, maybe even when I gain some distance, have risen above the intensity, that the first line, the right word suddenly presents itself. For no reason, it is suddenly there. This might happen in my sleep, or when I am doing something other than sitting staring fixedly at my iPad. Both it and I at an impasse. It's the first line of the poem that counts. That is the touchstone. That fuels the rest and it is the first line that provides the turbo charge I am looking for. I am then on my way and with work, the rest usually follows. Once the process begins the rest is like throwing a pot. It can take a few hours, days or even months and I am restive and unrelaxed until I am satisfied with what is there. Though that sense of completion is fleeting. Whatever is on the page is always work in progress. With perspective and the passing of time, there is always the possibility of improvement and change or even a complete redraft of published work.

The writing of prose is a slightly different matter. I have for now, a set pattern, scoping with words a rough cut of what I want to say and then I leave it to ripen overnight. At this point away from the text, the better words come, other additions or ideas flow in and on the next day and the days that follow, I read and reread what is there and write more from there. This drafting and redrafting, a cyclical process of going backwards and moving forwards, somehow releases the knots and opens the valves. With the wheel turning, the moulding, teasing, developing of what has started as ordinary clay, comes that euphoric feeling of spinning, tumbling, swimming through clouds and suddenly I am no longer in charge. In some way, it is I who am being shaped, me on that wheel, in a now giddy spin, and I have at times no idea what will appear on my screen but I know from deep within that for me, it's just right.

Besides the question of how I write, which often comes up at readings and events, is the other question about translation. Not long ago, I found myself having to, in a very limited time, publisher and printer in waiting, retranslate large chunks of my own book, around 13 of the 20 or so chapters. All I remember of fabulous Galicia last September, somewhere I had wanted to visit for a long time, because of its Celtic connections, is sitting in a park or else in a kindly café where I could work for hours with a slice of soft, moist tortilla and a glass of Albariño.

That identity switch from writer to translator was revealing. It brought about some interesting conundrums. For I suddenly found myself writing for a different readership, no longer an English speaking audience. This change of focus had me teetering on a pinpoint of cultural understandings and difference and sometimes as an Italian Scot, I was challenged as to where my loyalties lay. At times, I became more Italian and at others devotedly Scottish. Did I really want to enter into or invite light banter about the Italian canonical devotion to pasta with Italians? My Italian publisher certainly did not want me to! Where Luath was perfectly relaxed about my reporting of chocolate fetishes and the endemic, historic and pervasive attachment to fish and chips here in this country, did I really want to expose this elsewhere? Loyalty aside, there is much more to fish and chips than the food. It is not a 'fish dinner' or *'una cena a base di pesce'*; the after-pub rituals of it, the snooty newspaper wrapped presentations of it in well stacked parts of Scotland; or the sitting on a wall watching boats in Anstruther or Elie while contentedly munching, tearing soft potato and crispy batter; or again the much more disturbing poke of chips for a child's tea and often he is too, sent himself to get them.

As I wrote, I found myself on the brink of launching into a tirade about child poverty in Scotland or the disgrace of the Highland Clearances, Scotland's devastation and forced urbanisation. I sharpened my thinking in order to explain to Italians, in precise terms, the governance of organisations, promotion structures, systems of educational provision; and I learned a lot too about the weight, heft and tone of words, their appropriacy when rendered in another language.

Most of all though, after much reflection and a great deal of perspiration I concluded that translation is much more than a mechanistic exercise. Not only does a translator need to fully inhabit the value system, philosophy and practices of a country, to imbibe and embrace it and its roots, but the act of translation is a highly creative act. In the intersections of word with word, one language with another, lies the wellspring for innovative thinking and a new energy for different readers with different mind sets and expectations; there is fodder there for more than a little genius and small acts of seduction.

It is October 2018 and I am sitting in the front row of the performance area in the Scottish Storytelling Centre in Edinburgh's Old Town; my daughter Roberta is beside me with her guitar. On the screen on stage is a blown-up photo of my grandparents and family. There is a copper kettle on a table. Around 60 people who have come and paid money, to listen for an hour or so, are waiting to hear me tell a story, read and even, sing. Which surprisingly I do. I croon an old tune of my grandmother's.

The Billie Holiday introduction stops, and we mount the stage. I had never ever dreamed, never imagined that I would do anything like this one woman show.

Approach and technique apart, by far the most significant events of *Language* took place over the following two years. An outcome I had neither planned nor anticipated. For me rather unexpectedly, the book together with my first collection of poems in *Transitory* (Luath Press, 2018) evolved. It became something else. From words on a page, the book became a live dynamic, a tool, a very welcome starter for a conversation – a conversation which for some people was much needed. From Skye to Dundee, to Florence, to Glasgow, in libraries, in bookshops as well as in the high spots of the Edinburgh arts venues, I shared the messages and the experiences. Those connections and exchanges across the hall, in groups and as têtes-à-têtes were precious. The emails, personal messages and stories told to me personally went beyond any sense of achievement, nomination or aspiration to literary merit. We talked about mother daughter relationships; we talked about family, about support and toxicity; we talked about loneliness; we discussed abuse, domination and power.

And we laughed a lot too.

While preambles, the thinking behind my story, the proud tale of the Italians in Scotland was important to share, for me and for my family too, it was the intimacies and the communities of practice, all of us learning from each other as part of a joint endeavour, that became the foreground of readings and events. In these places the book found its voice. It lived and breathed in moving, heart-warming, challenging and very humbling words. These were people and experiences, this was an honesty that I will not forget. My objective is always honesty. Like the good biographers before me, I am impatient with discretion. And together with that honesty, a deep faith in possibility, in our resourcefulness as human beings, our toughness, our ability to push on through, to remake, to live many, many lives in a lifetime. On the front cover of the paperback version of *Language* is a painting by a talented and celebrated Scottish artist, Scott Naismith. Its title is *Optimistic Path*.

Marcus Coates, a contemporary artist with an interest in contrasting man-made processes with the natural world inscribes his work in *The Extended Mind* exhibition (Talbot Rice Gallery, Edinburgh, November 2019 to February 2020) as an illustration of 'how our interactions with other people can extend our own minds'. Any open engagement between people I believe, can, not only extend our minds but it can extend our emotional range too. It can broaden and enhance our vocal and experiential range as well. Writing as a space for discussion, and music and the visual arts has a unique ability – a capacity to hit you in the gut, to loosen, dislodge, uproot what might have been silenced through shame, fear, embarrassment, lack of confidence and self-belief for many years. This catharsis is an important function of creative outputs and a precious, healing and ultimately inspiring event for us all; for those who put it out there and those who enter the discussion. In a world of increasingly diminishing resources, funds for the arts are limited. Writers, poets, musicians, artists live in a highly competitive, volatile world, sometimes on a cliff-edge, anxious to catch the eye of the gatekeepers, the bookshops, the publishers, the curators of galleries and live performances – concerned up until the very last about whether the book will actually get to print, the poem appear (for there are never guarantees), the curtain will rise or whether the horn player will be up to his solo for your song on the night.

While I cannot deny the commercial imperative, I believe that irrespective of what values and preoccupations, what imagery, machinations and imaginations inform public taste and consumption, make up the list on concert programmes, fill the Edinburgh galleries, line the bookshelves, our main concern as writers is not those things. Ours is not to follow but to innovate and challenge. Not for us to imitate, to please and appease and never to conform. It is ours to speak candidly with all the skill and energy, all the passion that we can muster, in every corner we can find, invited or not invited. We all, as creatives and writers from every area of society, as young black women, as people with disabilities, as both older and younger women and men – (let none of us be overlooked in the hustings) for each of us beautiful or not, cool or not, undecorative or supreme, has a valuable perspective, in our authentic voices, to offer our fellow human beings. As a new writer and poet, I feel I have much more I want to share. I want many more conversations about self-belief, opportunity and adventure and it is for this reason that I am writing this new book.

Goro Murayama, a Japanese graphic designer who was also shown in *The Extended Mind* exhibition, writes interestingly that 'human error which will inevitably creep into such a work... contributes to the evolution of the creative process'.

No one completes a book or a poem with the idea that it is perfect, and at the end, when the final sentences are in place, there is no euphoria; only, at least for me, maybe a feeling of bewilderment and a strong awareness of imperfection; of the thought that much could be better. Nevertheless, irrespective of my own limitations, the challenges that I confront regarding my own creativity and writing skills, my errors even, and irrespective of the very variable, Tantric blessings of any queen or king maker, magic wand, talent scout, arts reviewer or stylish gatekeeper, what I have set out here is both an invitation and an exhortation.

variations

... at a chamber concert very recently, listening with unexpected pleasure to one of Beethoven's first piano trios I had the sudden, alarming realisation that I would die with so much music inside me never developed, never made, never found or even imagined. Throughout my life music has been an underground continual stream of bubbling white water at times; at others, a smoking, rich, unctuous lava stream. I was chilled at the thought. I began to reflect on a life lived with music, both the making of it and the listening to it; I realised in that brief moment of awakening, while continually aware of and alive to music in my home (the fun and hotch potch of my girls' instruments: oboe, cello, violin, saxophone, piano; their beloved *Lion King* and *The Sound of Music* soundtracks; early morning radio; in the car, and in venues around the city; in the street), I had often eluded its call and grasp. Not always did I invite it into my life, permit it to flood in. Yet like the constant lover who never gives up on you, sometimes after a little coaxing of stiff or misplaced fingers, adapting to fretboard or keyboard, seeking and eventually finding the key, it responded with overwhelming generosity, leaving me wondering why I had so often abandoned it.

There is no better example of the changing representations of who I am, of continual shift and enduring continuity – of the wandering spirit, and of aspiration, as fundamental threads and a core belief in my life – than music. My bond with music has been intimate: Harry James, Benny Goodman, Sinatra ballads and swing; Billie Holiday, Mahalia Jackson; Fats Waller and Sophie Tucker.

Then the discovery of the Beethoven Violin Concerto and operatic greats such as Caruso and Callas; the simple pleasure of Bach Preludes and Fugues, which I wrestled with as a teenager preparing for grade exams and which later brought so much pure joy. The Verdi *Requiem* that almost had me leapfrogging with sheer glee over the greyed genteel seated in the stalls of Edinburgh's Usher Hall, the Philip Glass concerto that nearly made me crash the car. The love arias of Puccini's *La Bohème* which brought so many tears gushing that I had to pull over into a lay-by. These had all preoccupied me to near obsession as I sought out other music by Glass, dragged friends to local jazz festivals, travelled to London to hear more Puccini at the Royal Opera House, sang with any choir that was preparing a Verdi piece for a concert and then put aside in favour of a career move, a new baby, a holiday in Italy, a new language or more recently again, the writing of my first book and the planetary shift that it brought about. Before the book, I identified as a musician who sometimes wrote a poem. The publication of that book has changed who I am, a writer who sometimes attends orchestra rehearsals and who practises too rarely.

From the age of 13 until 31, when I had my first baby, music and mainly piano, was central to how I conducted my life. Music was the productive, carefree space of adventure and fun around which all else was planned, considered and took place. I developed a foot-tapping liking for what was in the charts or on *Top of the Pops* that kept me jogging along at times when I was less than serious or wanted to float. I gathered together a few chords on the guitar and some notes on the recorder in order that I could play Christmas carols and bring my French and Italian teaching to life.

These forays were mere musical asides however. The bloodline of emotion, lonely and lyrical, blank and bewildered, tender and sweet, ferocious and strident was the piano: Beethoven, Mozart, Chopin, Debussy, fiery Albéniz, the dreaded Clementi. In my youth I had considered musical arrangement and conducting as an alternative to being a pianist. In school, I had amused myself by taking some well-known songs and arranging them for a two-part female choir. In my early teaching years, I formed a choir and briefly took charge of music in my parish church, until I found that the Saturday night preparations impinged too much on my social life, which was beginning to warm up. Those were too, the days of French folk songs brought fresh from my time spent in France to the classroom. There were organ lessons too which abruptly stopped when my amazing teacher was knocked down and killed crossing Princes Street. I joined a prestigious Edinburgh choir and sang in the staff choir at school. When a jazz band formed, made up of staff and pupils, a colleague arranged for me to have a few drumming lessons so that I could give some crowd-pleasing welly to 'cool' liturgical events for teenagers.

One of my guilty pleasures was to turn up the sound

on my music player at home and conduct a symphony. It wasn't the public spectacle that I sought, but the being in and with music. Pencil in hand (my conductor's baton), orchestra imagined and arrayed before me, with no score and only my memory of the different parts and entries, I stood for the entire piece waving my arms, encouraging and soothing, enlivening, drawing the best, most eloquent, purity or savage sound from my musicians, for a good half hour or so. In my early 20s, I sometimes couldn't wait to get home from teaching and to start up the concert. It would take me over so entirely, that everything disappeared into the flow of notes and harmonies, the vagaries and character of the different orchestral instruments.

This private musical extravaganza suddenly stopped for a while when I became a busy career mother. I was no longer a musician or indeed a pianist. The house music of family life took over, its soundtrack, The Singing Kettle's 'I'm Being Eaten by a Boa Constrictor', 'Aiken Drum', 'Bunny Fou Fou'; Phil Collins, Queen, Abba, Jackson, Punk Rock and the like, and sometimes all of these at once, from different areas of our house. In retreat, unable to compete, I made no more music. I was no longer productive, expressing any creative energy and aspiration in my work or in the risottos or bean stews I presented on the family dinner table. I would of course play along at Christmas, bring friends and family together for singalong carols, get the guitar out, but I had lost so much musical technique and verve, lost so much of my connection with music itself, that I was reluctant to expose even what I knew well or settle into a symphony late at night.

I resumed my piano playing and former self when

the girls were a little older in the late '80s and found a teacher who could put up with sometimes little practice and late cancellations. He brought me back, the old me of once upon a time, finding huge areas that needed development, re-establishing now, my wavering musical instinct and intuition. For several months, in the late evening when the girls were sleeping, I worked hard at getting back to the technical demands of my instrument, gradually regaining that intimacy and familiarity that comes with time and struggle. But this revival lasted a short while before career and family claimed me again.

Had there only been a little more time in the day I realise, how much a cello suite, a Palestrina madrigal or a Boccherini quintet would have helped with those life challenges, including the death of my mother. Music would have helped with the sadnesses and underscored the many moments of jubilation. But I had lost interest in what music might offer mainly because in a time of turbulence, change and the unknown, settled meditation and reflection are very much needed but not a first thought. However, those Saturday morning piano lessons, the challenges and optimism that an hour with a teacher gave me, led to my first real appreciation of the Romantic piano repertoire. The desolate, seeking notes of Chopin's nocturnes, the thunder and wildness of his mazurkas and polkas, gave me back temporarily a bit of an identity lost and revealed an authentic other.

In my late 30s I felt the call again. The surge was too great to resist. Wiser now, knowing that too much time and effort were required to make a serious return to the piano, I started going to concerts, renewing an old habit of season tickets and a fortnightly commitment.

I became a simple consumer. This was the time for Mozart and after more life experience of loving and lust, my yearning for the kind of love that I did not have, of sheer frolicking, I saw in that music what had been denied to me before; and I relaxed into horn concertos, flute and harp and bassoon concertos, violin concertos and the full set of piano concertos and sonatas. This was glorious! The transition from the spare scoring of JS Bach so adored in my ascetic, virginal years, to the rich blossoming and harmonic fullness of Mozart in my spice-seasoned later years, blew me away. In not making music and in listening, maybe, released from the burden of unattainable perfection, I was all the more ready to fall into it. I found too that this classical paradigm of strict form, of mere suggestion and a semblance of emotional order, of eloquent, elegant narratives of fear and dread; passion and tenderness in sweet repose; unruly play, both tantalised and delightfully teased. That 'falling' for Mozart's canon took me to a second stage in my relationship with music and I requested a cello for my 40th birthday.

After a year or two of being a cellist, I knew that the instrument could never be what the piano, my childhood friend and support, the soft ground of all my worries and joys, was or had been to me. We struggled on, the cello and I, through the demands of my career – I was moving away into more senior and national roles necessitating travel. I did achieve a standard at which I was able to play along in a few local orchestras. But my hopes for a kind of Second Coming, an instrument that would speak for me, that would connect with the heady rush of the gush and grain of me were never realised. I often arrived breathless and bothered at rehearsals having worked the day, travelled, cooked and dispatched, at a lesson or a rehearsal with my instrument badly tuned, missing the required score or plainly late. Not being sufficiently prepared as to the required bowing often meant that my bow travelled in the opposite direction to that of my fellow players: poking those on either side of me, causing some physical discomfort and embarrassment; some shifting of position or indeed seats and so I took to positioning myself at the end of a row. My love of and grasp of music was never seen, had been lost in a sea of important inconsequentials and I was no less than truly humiliated. With great shame I confess that The Really Terrible Orchestra, of Edinburgh Fringe fame and Alexander McCall repute, would not have me back. And I am sure that the Colinton Orchestra, where a great deal of tiresome scraping characterised the night, were also glad to see me gone.

And so for many years I settled for being an ardent music consumer. One however, who I admit has a sense of herself, 'opinionated' probably, to the annoyance of musicians and certainly to anyone who dares venture any kind of strong adverse opinions on music. There are few areas in life where I feel certain of my position and view, but music is most surely up there. I might even refer unthinkingly to the insistence or persistence of minimalism as in Adams' operatic output; or the sermonising of some of James MacMillan's work. And I find myself expressing personal loss and sadness at professional playing without personality or rawness, at any over-professionalisation of something which requires significant content, which begs questions or confronts; which because of a preoccupation with technical brilliance fails to articulate or set free what we didn't even know was there.

In 1967, days before my grandmother's death, I was taken to the opera twice in the same week as part of a school outing and saw *Madame Butterfly* and then Mozart's wicked and rather more playful and satirical *Don Giovanni*. From sparse, somewhat random beginnings, my relationship with opera took root. It offers the emotional explosion and unfolding, that baroque distils into something much purer and other-worldly. Taken together as a life-enhancing experience, for me they cannot be matched.

It was some years later however that I fell victim to melodrama and catharsis. Not for me the intellectual complexities of Wagner, the lore and language of it, the atonality, the monologues, the ponderous immutability and rootedness of it, nor indeed the sandwich, flask and supper rituals and dialogues surrounding it. In London at the Royal Opera House not many years ago, having joined a queue that morning for a 'Friday Rush' ticket and being deliriously happy to have secured one, I found myself face-to-face that evening with a synopsis of Wagner's *The Flying Dutchman* about ten minutes before the start. It seemed to me interesting and indeed a wise strategy to announce forthcoming events and how positively tempting to offer such detail. Doubt mounting, however, I thought I would just check with the steward that I was indeed about to see Mozart's *Così Fan Tutte*. She confirmed instead that Wagner was indeed imminent. As I headed for the door, she called me back and with warm encouragement persuaded me to stay. In my rush and fluster that morning I had not thought to ask what opera I was booking for, but having decided to draw a red line at the end of Act One, I found to my surprise that I did stay for the entire performance, enjoyed the whole theatre of it. I may even have got to my feet during the overwhelming applause at the end of the performance. I have returned to ROH many times and it has been a highlight, music aside; a wonderful, glamorous splurge of *civiltà* and champagne through the years.

'Un Bel Dí, Vedremo' sung by the wonderful, though in my heretical view, thin-voiced Callas was my first awakening to this genre at the age of 14; a single or 45 RPM bought for me by my mother who rightly preferred the fuller- warmer-voiced Renata Tebaldi. While Mozart, Monteverdi, Britten and indeed Wagner require immense technical skill, what is even more important in the Donizettis, Bellinis and of course Puccini and Verdi I believe, is emotional content and contrast, radiant joy, all eclipsing passion, verve, strength, savagery and feral woman as in Bartoli's performance of the opera *Norma* in 2016 at the Edinburgh International Festival.

I was brought up in a home where jazz had been supreme. Where in many ways, my mother showed aspects of who she was in a way that she declined to exhibit elsewhere in her daily life. That music seemed to wring from her a longing and excitement that I did not normally see. And it moved her to words that were eloquent and honest. These open revealing moments, emotional points of connection, where I found something I constantly sought from my mother, led me to seek my own directions in jazz. Maybe it was his early versions of 'Chicago' or his vocals with Jo Stafford and The Pied Pipers singing 'I'll Never

Smile Again' that electrified me about Sinatra I can't quite recall, but there started a love affair; a significant relationship that has lasted throughout my life. In my loveless, hopeful years he sang 'Try a Little Tenderness' and 'I've Got Crush on You' to me alone; in carefree mood I sang along to 'Goody Goody', 'I Get a Kick Out of You', 'Pennies From Heaven'; in love, I listened to 'Misty' and 'That Old Feeling', 'How Deep is the Ocean'; and in gentle or sad mode, I felt the desolation of, indeed identified with him as he croaked 'One For My Baby' or quietly intoned, in simple unadorned notes, 'Are You Lonesome Tonight'. And when caught up in the process of falling in love: 'You Make Me Feel So Young' and 'It's Only a Paper Moon'. In my teens I was part of the Rat Pack; in front of the living room mirror I perfected his phrasing of 'All of Me', 'All the Way', 'They Can't Take That Away From Me' and 'High Hopes'.

But the song that leaves me speechless every time I hear it is 'Ol' Man River' where Sinatra's breathing is something that I have never heard before or since... one deep, prolonged and swooping note that would match the Queen of the Night's best in Mozart's *The Magic Flute* any day. To say that I enjoyed Sinatra or liked him, appreciated his singing would be an understatement. I inhabited every song, was present at every 'crap game' or candlelit dinner that I gathered photos of, from *Melody Maker* and *The New Musical Express*... made scrapbooks and pored over every one. And I never judged him when he smashed the camera of press photographers, was reported to have fired a gun into the vacant bed Ava Gardner and he had shared or when he called on Mafia cartels to put him back on the stage after his singing career crashed. In fact, in his position, it seemed to me the right thing to do.

I saw him sing in person eventually, when he visited Glasgow in 1990. I remember piercing blue eyes, those oh so familiar hand gestures on the long, sustained notes and I thrilled and cried because he was still after all the years, singing just for me.

and final notes...

... one crisp autumn morning in 2011, I set out to find a group of Edinburgh music makers that I had read of on Google. Retired now, time was on my side, my musical life would be all that it had not been before. I was also in the midst of a marital separation which opened up possibility. As I walked past Turkish and Indian takeaways, Italian restaurants and tenements in the Dalry area of Edinburgh, I suddenly heard a bagpipe and the ringing tremolo of mandolins. There were whistles too and other instruments that I couldn't identify. I followed the music and walked straight into a church where my eyes met those of the legendary Nigel Gatherer, composer, arranger, a master – as I later came to appreciate – of Scots traditional music and father of generations of whistle and mandolin players. There he was, pleasantly and patiently leading the band. I sat listening, overawed, smiling and utterly delighted.

'Can I help you?' he asked when they stopped playing.

'Yes,' I said, 'Can I play music with you?'

The following Wednesday I returned with a cello in tow or in reality, on my back and played on open strings. I was rusty to say the least, providing a sort

I am always doing that which I cannot do, in order that I may learn how to do it.

(Pablo Picasso)

of unlikely pibroch effect for the next fortnight or so. The instrument was unwieldy, I had forgotten most of what I knew. But each time I went to that Wednesday class, although I was all too conscious of limitations, I felt the beginnings of a kind of wholeness again, a return of an abandoned self.

Then, in a frustrated and discontented frame of mind one day, I wandered into a shop selling a dazzling array of instruments. As is always the case, I wanted most of what I saw. It was only after exploring carriage charges and the practicalities of flying a Portuguese guitar home from Porto that I gave up on the idea of buying one although that dream still remains as a possibility. In this music shop in Edinburgh, I was suddenly rooted to the spot, lovestruck no less. There it was, very humbly hanging on a wall: a plain, pale wood, neither shiny or outspoken, little mandolin. Tasteful, understated.

Before asking the price, wee mando and I, had agreed our own terms. Putting behind me the guilt and shame of my cello experience, which I had fancied would give voice to the soulful and melancholy in me, and resisting the sense of betrayal towards my beloved but now London-dwelling piano (since I had finally handed it over to my daughter), I paid for the mandolin and took it home. It sat teasingly on its stand at the foot of my bed for a few weeks.

Finally, ignoring any misgivings about starting another musical project which might again take second place to a life change, I committed to some lessons. These weeks of learning the new sound system of a plucked instrument, each string with its own character and offering of notes; of quite a brisk entry to and engagement with a kind of music that for me, captures the essence of what it is to be or feel Scottish, set my bones a booming and the hairs on the back of my neck bristling. It was no less than utterly thrilling. To play with other people, a new experience for a pianist, many of whom I discovered, were like-minded, shared the same political ideals as I did (the same passion and pride in our Scottish culture), opened up, defined and made solid an aspect of my identity and beliefs which I had not been aware of before. But besides the sense of fellowship, I also felt a sense of rootedness, of home and belonging.

I had felt the same sense of arrival and bonding, a kind of being in the right place and deep pulsating in my veins, lump in my throat, at the sound of the old Neapolitan songs, songs in a dialect that I grew up with: Massimo Ranieri, Aurelio Fierro and even Lou Monte with 'Peppino the Little Mouse'! Both musics move me to tears. Both seem to claw at the depths of me, rendering me incoherent, unable to explain. To have the same sense of 'my people', of hearth and heartedness with two very different ethnic groups, both Scottish and Italian, and with two different languages, vernacular and dialect, two different traditions and histories, yet both expressing the heart of a people, oppressed and proud, dashing, esoteric and characterful, yearning after a shared vision and societal ideology; untamed and unrefined, as animal as any voiced, visceral flamenco, is unsettling and yet weirdly enriching.

The mandolin has brought many things to my life: the pints, the pubs and the dark room experiences, the jokes and the ribaldry, the makeshift and the make do; the fumbling and the, at times, pretences of chord shifts and key change; the constant encouragement of friends and colleagues for what you can do and not what you can't; the feeling that what is in hand is a joint endeavour, that perfection is not in our vocabulary, maybe not even within reach.

The mandolin has brought me that truly wonderful orchestral experience that I always sought, in concert halls, in any country that I have visited and in front of a mirror in my own living room. There are times at orchestra rehearsals, for I now have a commitment to an ever aspiring and rather excellent plucked instrument ensemble (with serious and talented players), when I know that we have gone beyond notes, beyond technique and fluency to quite simply producing fine music. There is that sense of movement upwards and forwards, and like the machair of some lonely place in the Hebrides, of blending and synchronicity and of total oneness.

In London, in Kings Cross tube station recently, I heard the sound of a mandolin and the words of a song that I learned to play on a piano in an Italian village at the age of 17: 'Catarì' echoed through the halls as people rushed by, and overcome, reluctant to walk on, wanting to put my arms around the busker from my own area of Italy, and with that same sense of home far and away, my heart still pounding, I stepped on to the train to Scotland, to my Edinburgh and to a fiddle lesson on Saturday morning! A new beginning, a new journey. A new challenge, success or failure. All of it is living and the day's promise.

Paganini, Elgar, Haydn, Corelli, the composers who have blessed generations with 'Variations on a Theme' are too numerous for me to list. Schubert's iconic 'Trout Quintet' is an outstanding example evoking shimmering, leaping fish as they twist and turn in bubbling waters. Closer to our own times, composers of this form of music include John Williams' 'Variations on Happy Birthday', John Cage's 'Hymns and Variations' and Andrew Lloyd Webber who wrote 'Variations for cello and rock band' in 1977. The first set appeared in the 14th century, but this musical form, of exposition followed by diverse iterations of an original melody, became fashionable later in the 16th century. Virtuosi of the piano or violin display their technical brilliance and creative skill by improvising variations on a tune to ecstatic receptions from their audiences. In a sense, the soaring dramas of musical cadenzas in concertos for solo instruments as well as jazz improvisations are not too far from this musical form either. Variations on a central theme can be melodic, rhythmic, harmonic or the same tune in a minor key which can radically change the mood.

The central theme in this piece is that of undaunted, relentless aspiration. Underlying every new approach to music, learning another instrument, to the shift from music maker to consumer; from a life of smooth ooze of a Dorsey trombone and scat-singing Fitzgerald or Cab Calloway to the Well-Tempered Clavier or the 48 of JS Bach, from Sinatra madness to operatic coloratura to the nose dive into the romantic cliché and predictability of Verdi and Puccini from the fascinating draw of 12th century hymns by Hildegard von Bingen, is a restless, urgent and immoveable will to experience in whatever way, all the music, all its facets and richness, all its moods and tonalities that there is and has been. More importantly, this piece essentially about variability, articulates the central unchanging self on a core mission towards adventure, the new and untried.

There are many opportunities for us to evolve, to grow, to learn. We can choose or are sometimes drawn by some instinctive, irrepressible urge to circumstances where we can fully shine, become brighter, bring to light what has been overshadowed or discover and even create ourselves anew, an identity the brilliance of which we had never even imagined: Carmen Herrera, a Cuban artist, now 104, only sold her first painting 15 years ago, when she was 89. She has been dubbed a female genius whose recognition still grows and whose first show took place in New York in 2016.

This is my personal hymn to music. It is also a metaphor for life; how, as adaptable, open people we approach the life flow of happenings and events, the daily demands; how we take up challenges and create challenges for ourselves; how we overcome difficulties, make compromises, accept failures, and enjoy the full impact of success.

This is a tale about how we contend with who we know we are, imagine who we would like to be and what strategies we can construe that might take us there. Like Herrera, a testament it is said, to the power of consistency, we never give up on our plan to journey for the better.

As learners, we welcome every teacher in our long lives. Many come from unexpected places. Through those words or ideas that we exchange, those collaborations and shared insights, we expand, become taller, grander and more fully human with a new focus, perspective and altered aspirations. Like variations on a central, consistent tune we find that our interconnections are as melodic, rhythmic or harmonic as those 'Variations on a Theme' by Paganini, where through every deviation and derivation, enhancing the original musical statement, the throbbing core theme is heard still but in magnificently and appealingly different presentations.

We should always be aware of and use the force of self-creation because that is what makes us human. We should never abandon or ignore our innate powers and sustained energy. We should continually reinstate our unwavering, instinctive lust for life. It is that undercurrent that carries us through. That ebb and flow of a lava stream is our enduring will always to greet each day, to rise and fill the hours, to move forward, explore, try, retry and become. For as makers, we are master builders in the project of self-making.

tailpiece

... have you ever heard the steady breathing of someone else when you are alone in a room? From time to time I hear it. I hold my breath to be sure. But there it is, rhythmic, reliable, even and deep. I listen again. Who is that? Could it be me? A sleeping me, yet to be awakened? Some discarded me from years, from yesterday, from last night? An unwanted former presentation of me and my lifestyle; a daily pattern that fixed me, trapped me; made me suddenly predictable even to myself; removed surprise and wonder from my life? Or is it the unwritten me? The me I will be today; the me I set out to be this morning and the me that the world, the day, routine intrusions will form and mould and whom I will greet at the day's end. 'Hello and who are you now?' Was it the book that you picked up on a whim, in a radical bookstore that refocused you and made you face in another direction? Was it the poster you saw in the coffee shop about paths to happiness, or a talk on philosophy and politics and Plato's truths? Was it the Facebook invitation to trek the Cévennes on a donkey, RL Stevenson style, that made you check your diary? Was it the woman at the gym who had just come back from a meditation retreat on the pebbled beaches of a Greek island? Or maybe that person somewhere beside you and whose breath echoes yours, is the person that will write a trilogy; take up boxing; cycle in Sweden for which I gather, you do not need to be either super fit or mega rich; or take to the streets and provide haircuts to homeless men.

Each separate section of this book expresses a central intention like 'Variations on a Theme'. To put into words, to communicate, to represent hope, opportunity and possibility. They are all underpinned with a firm conviction that whatever life offers is a chance to grow; a firm belief in the richness of life and excitement at all the world and people have to offer. Within each frame, the bold curves, tonal suggestions, sometimes the straight unbroken lines, redrawing of our human experience is somewhere to be found. Through a range of emotions and openness, indecision and purposefulness, resolve and struggle, failure and success, retreat and striding out, I always have the continuous will to move on in hope and trust in better.

In order to truly live, we must feel free. Despite what is around us, we must feel that we can manoeuvre. We must find that space and those gaps. The master key to evolution and rebirth, to continual growth, personal revolution even, lies in our intellectual freedoms; how we see ourselves; how free we feel. Only through the feeling of being free, unconstrained, and limitless can we be open to and grasp; change and become; be limitless, believe that we are. The quietly confident seizing of personal power cannot fail.

Simone de Beauvoir famously wrote 'I wish that every human life might be transparent freedom'. Jacques Derrida, the French philosopher, wrote 'I do everything possible or acceptable in order to escape from this trap'. Closer to home, Stephen Fry has famously described himself as a 'lover of truth and a worshipper of freedom'. Freedom, or the extent to which we each of us feels they have the power to move, to reorientate, to change their personal circumstances and live another life, is often dependent on a number of practical, societal or personal barriers. Often the obstructions are just too great; they are financial, structural, cultural; they are embedded in the society we live in. History records the impact of politics on silenced Irish Catholics; on women; on the frustrations of the people of Catalonia. We stand by and watch the anguish of citizens in Venezuela, trapped by the vagaries of a political regime; food and medicine in short supply; and on our streets we are confronted daily with the effects of government policy, of ineptitude and callousness in practice with the need for food banks and people begging in freezing temperatures. We see or read about these cataclysms, atrocities; about the silenced, the disappeared, the powerless and other injustices. We are passionate, hungry even in our endeavours to do whatever we can to help.

Overcoming the barriers that we ourselves face may not quite rock the stability of our homeland or lead to civil war but they are still significant and they still require immense courage and even personal loss. We all face barriers of some kind and at some time; factors that frighten us, cause anxiety, anger us, crush, disempower and prevent us from moving on.

As an older writer, sometimes with other, different things to say, I often feel discounted: invisible both as a woman and as someone with some mileage. As a young professional I experienced prejudice of various kinds and even bullying, more than once. As a mother I certainly confronted despair. I have been well supported in my efforts and I have been surrounded by heartless negativity which has made me weep. My shaky beginnings, through my work and in my personal life convince me however, that nothing is beyond us; that freedom, opportunity and possibility are all available and that there is always a way.

I have never understood impossibility, never accepted rejection though I have lived with it, endured it and suffered through it at times. I have never understood the barriers that challenged me. I do not accept them as fixed. We can always be more than we ever believed possible and it's the willing shift, the openness, the trying, the endeavour, the implacable and cast iron positivity and the vision that makes us grow; makes us fully, wonderfully and most happily human.

Scanning the planet we see continual structural and ideological change, societal reorganisation, an interconnected world. Never has the need for individualism, to grasp the opportunities that universal change offers us, to self-make as new norms and pressures to conform settle around and upon us, been more real.

In the spaces left by the uprooting of the old and the rerooting of new cultures, our own agency, our own compass in our self-making journey is paramount if we are not to live our lives as an artefact, a mere embodiment of social norms and cultural practices that are not our own.

We construct our own narrative. These self-created versions of ourselves are where both our own fulfilment lies and the future of a diverse, open, equal and learning world. Our personal way forward lies in the hand that reaches out; the power of a message, inspiration from learning, from a political philosophy, from social media; we are motivated by gatherings of those with common purpose, by projects, by social movements and trends and the endless flow of information and knowledge through technology. Through the loopholes of those dialogues, of inner processes and openness, of knowledge and understanding, the possibilities are both real and endless.

To put it another way, in the words of one commentator, what is required is 'a way of being in the world, a way of constructing an identity for oneself that is different from, and arguably opposed to, the idea of belonging to or devotion immersion in a particular culture' (Waldron)… this 'cosmopolitanism represents a process of evolution; it is essentially a practice which is personally transformational and which has the effect of transforming relationships between individuals which ultimately has the potential to create change within the broader scope of society'.

The spider builds her own web; she does it unaided; her web is intricate, complex and often extensive. She has sole responsibility for both her web and her life's direction. Each web is complete, a new creation. She alone determines where it should be, where to locate herself. She determines its shape and spread, the relative thickness of each fibre according to usefulness and capacity to lure and keep her prey; and how much freedom to manoeuvre is available to her within that space. The important thing is to survive and with that basic requirement as her compass, on a whim or because of other factors outwith her control, she decides how long she stays in one place; moves on again and again, destroying her web often by eating it, and leaving no trace of herself. Nothing of her is left behind. Each time she moves, she builds again; starts all over again; her life a continuous cycle of building, creating and nesting anew. It and she are a constant reconstruction, a continual process of mutation and adaptation.

Spiders are capable of creating great beauty. Their artistry and craft are astonishing. Their senses always on high alert, reacting to every movement, sound and change of air. In every place that they inhabit they are immensely productive. From their natural resources, their genetic code and heritage, they create copious yarn of the finest silk, and endless, streaming, light-filled gossamer. As individuals, we have that same innate ability to create around us that same magic, that capability for what is supernatural, beyond the bounds of human capacity, that can make our lives, not only valuable or meaningful, but an existence never before imagined. We are capable of great and small acts of importance, significance, grace and beauty.

While my everyday requires the energy to fulfil what is for me always an aspiration, there are and have been many days of immense struggle, I know and trust all the same, that we can make history and build futures. I believe that we can always be more than we are.

It is not the spiders who lie in wait for us. Our histories, experiences, whatever life throws at us, need not oppress us or darken all the years we have ahead. They will only do that if we allow them. We learn from these and believe in better. For what lies in wait for us are the years, the endless opportunities that each day offers, that each place presents and that the person that we might meet on a chance encounter can give us. What illuminates the sky in the brightest of colours, what makes the earth warm and the sea keep singing is the never ending, driving thrust for more, for better, for what else is available; for what else awaits.

… then along came a spider

my 'lockdown' has been gradual and progressive. Not long after I began editing this book, coronavirus gathered momentum here in the UK. We had already witnessed the horrors of what was ahead of us in China, Spain, Italy. As I write, those images on our television screens are being played out here at home. We hear tales of the rapid disposal of corpses with no witnesses present to prevent infection's spread. And I am reminded of my university reading of Camus' *La Peste* and Boccaccio's salacious *Decameron* written in the 14th century at the time when the Black Death was wiping out the Italian population. A group of men and women escaped to the countryside outside Florence and tell each other stories for ten days. But spring is not yet here and it would be cold on the hill outside the city. I guess too that I should be grateful for efficiency preventing rats.

I walk a deserted city centre. Our roads seem narrower somehow, silenced, stark and colourless with the absence of cars and people. The once beautiful neoclassical buildings of Edinburgh's New Town loom. Playfair and Adam architecture fill me with dread, reminding me of the Holy City and seem to suggest that I too, am one of the chosen. I am doomed. And tomorrow morning, I will wake up with that fever and racking cough which will feel like cracked glass. I take to the outdoors for an hour's worth of oxygen... three times around the local park each day. I vary the times when I go. I am not unable, but unwilling to go to sleep for fear of the next day. I have taken to listening to Haydn string quartets. They offer some order, some structure. The classical form is a familiar one and it offers a little reassurance. Last night I tried to listen to something new: Arvo Pärt. I found it too demanding, too disturbing. All I could visualise was walking alone in white space. After two minutes I stopped listening. And before venturing into the leafy, douce street where I live, masked and gloved, I arm myself for a possible brush with death, a surreal do-si-do with a passer-by which could prove lethal for either one of us. No one smiles. We fear each other.

I am chilled by daily feeds from NHS workers of people dying alone. No daughter to ease the passage, no outpouring of the visceral love that only mothers and daughters have; no girl of mine, whose comforting smell is so familiar, to hold me while I gasp for one more breath that will spin my life out just for a few minutes more; no last words before the threads of the umbilical cord that through all the years still tied us, finally dissipate. And I came to realise only very recently that 'keeping safe' is my only hope of ever seeing my children again. That is why I try and try.

This genocide perpetrated by a random quirk of nature, we are told, is what we are currently living through. A cull of our most vulnerable and our weakest. We question timing. We question political motives. We ask ourselves who is 'vulnerable' and by what criteria since like a cunning mass murderer, this virus is volatile, unpredictable, changing its MO as it sweeps across the globe. These issues are matters for historians and political theorists of the future. There are no answers as yet, and we are no match for this present-day pandemic. In the midst of it, I am finishing the writing of my book not knowing whether it will ever be read, what kind of world will greet it, or whether I or those I love will live to enjoy the fun and triumph of its publication it with me.

In each of these essays, I have described the lack of solidity and impermanence of everything in the universe including who we are. Change and shift in our material and spiritual, emotional and psychological worlds have been a major theme throughout. And now, a month ago in what seems like centuries, there was reliability. There was a kind of predictability about everything; even about change and futures. They were trackable to some extent. We anticipated, experts forecast, some of us even dared to imagine. But only days later, in this new unfamiliar habitat with much of what we know and took for granted gone, leaving only the bare minimum necessary, it feels, as though, if I allow myself to think it, the very firmament itself may collapse. So, I have retreated into a smaller world. The view outside my window is the same each day. The park is always there. I can connect to that other outside world which changes from hour to hour through my devices. I have some control over that. I have deserted social media and imposed a news blackout with no wish to hear the latest updates on numbers dead, no desire to hear that 'things will get worse'. I know the worst and news reaches me somehow anyway.

In this unpeopled landscape, the bark on my

sensibilities tree is altogether thinner, only a filmy covering now as I speak easily and naturally of love to not only family but to friends. I wave at strangers. I smile at children and dogs. The distance between both extremes of my emotional range has shortened. My veneers are prone to cracking, my voice is tear full, my cheeks are wet without warning. There is no build up, no signal in my intestine or my pulse rate. Apart from the irritations of those who ignore the rule about social distancing while walking, causing me often to leap fully clothed into the sea at Portobello or into the gutter in my local street. I love more freely and generously it seems. I appear at the moment, to love almost everyone. Each person is precious and every encounter is sweet. I give strangers who appear to want to engage, my full attention. I leave enriched.

Yet, as the virus barrelled towards our shores and the rapid lockdown to halt, or at least slow its pace, took root, there came other news. A cautious presence. The space between the headlines. A different kind of reporting. Glorious renewal. Precious good tidings. Please send us more. Cleaner air, the return of blue skies, clear water, reduced pollution. The drastic measures to reduce the impact of the pandemic have had a very real effect on the other even greater tragedy of global warming, and its devastating consequences. Faced with a stark and immediate choice, a small price to pay for our lives and the well-being of those we love, we willingly retreated into bare necessity, we embraced limitation, we freely subjected to a new kettling. We watch as the natural world, that unstoppable, creative energy that is its very essence, commences a tentative process of renewal.

For some time, many of us have had the uneasy feeling that the world was teetering on the edge of something; that things were badly out of control; that a kind of awakening was required; that we needed to rebuild our societies, our constitutions and historic institutions from basic foundations. That we urgently needed to rebuild the very fabric of human existence; and not least ourselves. Yet that collective hysteria, the grasping, the hunger, the pitting of human against human was too institutionalised and too endemic. The wave of Trumpism and his kind the world over, too great and powerful to hold at bay. The world is done with liberalism we were told. The old democratic order is for a dying generation.

Early indications are that, besides the unintended benefits of our actions on parts of the planet, something yet more radical in societal terms is afoot... a slight shift in our collective consciousness, a fundamental stirring, as yet unarticulated. In the changes to our individual lifestyles, as we wait out the passing of this catastrophe, there is maybe a profound human lesson that we are beginning to learn day by day, a new blueprint.

As we lock ourselves within and shut the door on the threat looming on the other side of it, we know with a new realism how fragile our own existence is; how powerless we ultimately are. We are aware of the preciousness of human life. We support the most vulnerable; we rely on others, and we see a world, our world, that functions on interdependence, on self-sacrifice on generosity. In the midst of death and fear of a lethal virus, people all over the world were spurred into action and protest at the callous murder of George Floyd. They 'took the knee' in solidarity and the Black Lives Matter movement shifted from rhetoric to real change. Someone still drives the ambulances, police look out for our security, pharmacists dispense our essential medication. Someone empties our bins, delivers our food, mail and essential parcels, drives the buses, sits at the supermarket check-out, cleans the trolleys, supervises the queues. Thousands have returned to the service of the NHS where doctors and medical staff put their lives at risk in order to care for the sick and dying. They do it because they want to help in whatever way they can. Local communities set up help networks, make contact with those unable to leave their homes. We telephone and talk to those we know have been shut away for weeks. We establish meaningful connections with spoken words; by listening; by sharing a joke, often with people we didn't really know: 'we will meet for coffee', 'come and visit... when it's all over, when we reach the other side'. We see more clearly that which connects us rather than our differences.

We adopt a new code of kindness; of compassion and care for those around us... in our neighbourhoods, streets, local shops. We say 'thank you' and we mean it. We really do. Mostly, we lay bare our innermost selves, examine our humanity. We move forward with a will and a belief in solidarity; ultimate faith in our ability to survive as individuals and a yearning for our society to be and to do better. We did not want this virus and we did not want this sudden change to the way we have always lived our lives. We did not seek tragedy, or fear.

The global pandemic stopped me in my tracks. My lifelong optimism, my belief in possibility, in individual freedoms, in the innate ability of humankind to upturn, manoeuvre, transform, the latent energy and power to withstand, survive and create suddenly in a matter of what seemed like hours, seemed to have no place. Happiness and joy belonged to a world that had been wiped out and with it the hope and ideals that I had founded a life and career on, that had suffused the music I had enjoyed, the writing I had found so rewarding; filled the fun-filled years while my children grew up.

But then that energy slowly returned. It increasingly shaped each day. I felt it at the first sign of spring and growth during lockdown. I felt its burst in early morning, amidst tall trees and strident birdsong. I felt it at the top of Edinburgh's Blackford Hill when the wind swallowed me up and shook me free of darkness and despair; when I managed to play my first fiddle tune and successfully bake a first loaf of bread. My thirst for life will always lead me on. Nothing will ever be quite the same.

As a society we have been through something momentous together. As individuals we have pitted our wits against something we have no understanding of; we have each of us made decisions about what we cherish most, how much our lives are of value and our chances of survival.

All of our relationships have in some way shifted position. We meet as survivors, family, friends and strangers too, with a new and common language and I am confident that the essence of this book, my faith in the human spirit, will resonate more fully and is more relevant now than even before.

Whatever and whenever is tomorrow, I believe that we will each individually and together in a common endeavour, regain and assert our freedom to choose and to allow nature's energy and power to renew, back into our precious Earth home and into our own lives.

We will choose another way.

further reading...

feminist writing

Beard, Mary, *Women and Power: A Manifesto*, Profile Books, 2017

Butler, Judith, 'On the culture wars, JK Rowling and living in 'anti-intellectual times', *New Statesman*, 22 September 2020

Cameron, Deborah, *Feminism*, Profile Books, 2018

Dickson, Anne, *The Mirror Within*, Quartet Books, 1985

Gay, Roxane, *Difficult Women*, Grove Atlantic, 2017

Hines, Sally, *Is Gender Fluid? A Primer for the 21st Century*, Thames & Hudson, 2018

Moran, Caitlin, *How To Be a Woman*, Ebury Press, 2011

Nagoski, Emily, *Come As You Are*, Scribe, 2015

Orbach, Susie *Fat is a Feminist Issue*, Virago, 2006 reissue

—*What's Really Going On Here? Making Sense of Our Emotional Lives*, Arrow, 1994 new edition

Penny, Laurie () *Bitch Doctrine: Essays for Dissenting Adults*, Bloomsbury, 2017

Piercy, Marge, *Woman on the Edge of Time*, Knopf, 1976

Solnit, Rebecca, *Men Explain Things To Me*, Granta, 2014

philosophy and other theory

Baudrillard, J, *Symbolic Exchange and Death*, Sage
    Publications, 1976

Bourdieu, Pierre and Passeron, Jean-Claude, *Reproduction in
    Education, Society and Culture*, Sage Publications, 1977

Foucault, M, *Power: The Essential Works of Michel Foucault
    1954–1984*, Penguin Modern Classics, 2020

Habermas, J, *The Structural Transformation of the Public
    Sphere*, Polity, 1962

hooks, b, *Teaching to Transgress: Education as the Practice of
    Freedom*, Routledge, 1994

Sarup, Madan, *Education, State and Crisis: A Marxist
    Perspective*, Routledge & Kegan Paul, 1982

identity

Holland, D, Lachicotte, W, Skinner, D, Cain, C (1998) *Identity
    and Agency in Cultural Worlds*, Harvard University Press

Giddens, A, *Modernity and Self-Identity*, Polity Press, 1991

Laing, RD, *Self and Others*, Penguin, 1990

Marková, I, *Dialogicality and Social Representations: The
    Dynamics of Mind*, Cambridge University Press, 2004

buddhist writing

Thich Nhat Hanh, *Touching Peace: Practising the Art of
    Mindful Living*, Parallax Press, 1992

Pema Chodron, *The Places That Scare You: A Guide to
    Fearlessness*, Harper Collins, 2003

The Dalai Lama *How to Practise: The Way to a Meaningful
    Life*, Ebury Press, 2002

other books

Harari, Yuval Noah, *A Brief History of Humankind*, Harvill Secker, 2014

Hazan, Marcella *The Essentials of Classic Italian Cooking*, Boxtree; Main Market Edition, 2011

listening... lockdown music

Lera Auerbach, Twenty Four Preludes for Violin and Piano; Vadim Glutzman (violin) and Angela Yoffe (piano)

Duncan Chisolm albums *Sandwood, canaich* and *affric*; and #COVIDCeilidh

Benedetti Sessions courtesy of The Benedetti Foundation

The Essential Philip Glass (Deluxe Edition) Philip Glass & The Philip Glass Ensemble

Haydn: The Complete String Quartets, Aeolian String Quartet

John Garth, Six Concertos for Violoncello, Tunnicliffe, Beznosiuk & Avison Ensemble

Bach: Goldberg Variations, Maisky, Caussé & Sitkovetsky

Some other books published by **Luath Press**

Language of My Choosing:
The Candid Life-Memoir of an Italian Scot
Anne Pia

PBK: £7.99 ISBN: 978-1-912147-39-7
HBK: £14.99 ISBN: 978-1-910745-91-5

Where do I truly belong? This is the question Anne Pia continually asked of herself growing up in the Italian-Scots community of post-World War Two Edinburgh.

This candid, vibrant memoir shares her struggle to bridge the gap between a traditional immigrant way of life and attaining her goal of becoming an independent-minded professional woman.

Through her journey beyond the expectations of family, she discovers how much relationships with other people enhance, inhibit and ultimately define self. Yet – like her relationship with her own mother – her 'belonging' in her Italian and Scottish heritages remains to this day unresolved and complex.

Transitory
Anne Pia
PBK: £7.99 ISBN: 978-1-912147-37-3

Anne Pia is a fresh voice among contemporary Scottish poets. The European context in which her imagination works, with poems responding to the work of Baudelaire, for instance, is taken as a given: Scotland and the community of European nations are mediated and represented in her poems with subtle understanding, sympathy and constructive insight, political realities that give 'nurture' to 'fledglings preparing to fly'.

ALAN RIACH

Through the poet's 'small and continuing dialogues', *Transitory* explores the ongoing state of change that we all inhabit. These intimate, elegant poems expose the impact of ourselves on the world, and the world on ourselves, touching on issues of identity, belonging and otherness with honesty and tenderness. From the Saltire Award shortlisted author of *Language of My Choosing*.

Details of these and other books published by Luath Press can be found at:
www.luath.co.uk

Luath Press Limited

committed to publishing well written books worth reading

LUATH PRESS takes its name from Robert Burns, whose little collie Luath (*Gael.*, swift or nimble) tripped up Jean Armour at a wedding and gave him the chance to speak to the woman who was to be his wife and the abiding love of his life. Burns called one of the 'Twa Dogs' Luath after Cuchullin's hunting dog in Ossian's *Fingal*. Luath Press was established in 1981 in the heart of Burns country, and is now based a few steps up the road from Burns' first lodgings on Edinburgh's Royal Mile. Luath offers you distinctive writing with a hint of unexpected pleasures.

Most bookshops in the UK, the US, Canada, Australia, New Zealand and parts of Europe, either carry our books in stock or can order them for you. To order direct from us, please send a £sterling cheque, postal order, international money order or your credit card details (number, address of cardholder and expiry date) to us at the address below. Please add post and packing as follows: UK – £1.00 per delivery address; overseas surface mail – £2.50 per delivery address; overseas airmail – £3.50 for the first book to each delivery address, plus £1.00 for each additional book by airmail to the same address. If your order is a gift, we will happily enclose your card or message at no extra charge.

Luath Press Limited
543/2 Castlehill
The Royal Mile
Edinburgh EH1 2ND
Scotland
Telephone: +44 (0)131 225 4326 (24 hours)
Email: sales@luath.co.uk
Website: www.luath.co.uk